stopped. I didn't know why, and I didn't care. I jumped up and raced to the shower. There, I scrubbed myself until parts of my skin were raw.

Later, he said not to tell Momma. He said that she would be jealous because she wanted him all to herself. I didn't understand what was wrong with that; I wanted him all to *herself* too!

It didn't matter what he said anyway. I wasn't going to keep quiet. I was going to do what I did best—talk!

We visited Momma in the hospital that day, but not before he took me out for breakfast and shopping for new clothes. None of this secured my silence.

I got Momma alone in the hospital visitors' lounge and told her everything. I felt so relieved that we were now moving on without him. I thought that maybe she could marry someone else who was not interested in little girls.

Momma went back to her room where he was while I waited in the lounge. The time she was away seemed long. I thought, she must really be getting him told!

What were they saying? What was going to happen? Were the police coming? Would I get to stay at the hospital with Momma?

Then, Momma returned.

She reported that the Reverend had sworn on a Bible in her room that he didn't do it, and that was good enough for her.

"He was willing to let you stay with him while I'm here, so don't f-ck it up!" Momma growled.

I went back home with Reverend Nasty. And he had his way with me—stealing my youth, my innocence, my virtue. As I lay numb, wishing for a savior, he did it again and again, day and night. Only now, he had permission from my mother.

On my first day back to school after being robbed and

violated, I told classmates, who told teachers. In a matter of minutes, I was ushered to the school social worker, who called the police. At the police station, I wasn't withdrawn or distraught in the least. In fact, I was quite cheerful while cooperating with Detroit's Finest. I felt safe. They were going to take care of everything. It happened, it was over, and I was confident that it wouldn't happen again.

The officer seemed tired as she took my statement. She was pretty, and I didn't understand why she was a police officer. *Why would anyone who had beauty risk losing it in the line of duty?*

I had been told I was ugly for years, and even though I didn't think I was that bad looking, I wondered how much better life would be if I were considered attractive by other people.

I wasn't yet developed and I was scrawny. I wore large, round, plastic Medicaid eyeglasses. The lenses were thick, overwhelming for my pea head, and slid down my nose all the time. I had long, lifeless hair that was braided on both sides—a style the old folks called "plats." It's fair to say that I was the ideal poster child for inner-city homeliness.

As the officer continued to type, I told her all about how Reverend Nasty had invited himself to pinch my one swollen nipple that up until then only Momma had seen. I told her about him bragging that he did the same things to his biological daughter, Tiffany, who was eight at the time. I told the officer about the dirty magazines he showed me, and how he bit my "private" and made me cry. I told her that he threatened to *really* take "it" from me when I turned eighteen because he said that Momma would probably be dried up or dead.

I felt good about telling the officer the truth, so I told it all. I talked and talked until everything had been said.

I believed that even if no one else had ever been concerned about me, I mattered to the police. They didn't care if I was "bad" or that I talked so much. They weren't mean to me because I didn't have the right clothes. They weren't preoccupied with worshiping the Provider, and they weren't confusing me with a million other kids who had names that begin with "Er."

Hours passed. The policewoman had now blended back in with her colleagues and was working on other things. I watched as officers walked around, chatting, chewing, sipping and carrying paperwork. Their footsteps, while competing with the ringing phones, echoed loudly throughout the hollow halls of the large historic building. My bottom was numb from sitting on the hard bench, and my empty stomach sounded like the static from the officer's walkie talkies. I had missed lunch while sitting with the school counselor waiting for the police earlier, and I hadn't had breakfast, so I asked for food.

The police told me that my grandparents had been called and were on the way. I wasn't sure how that solved my problem as much as it added to it. It would be hours before I would have my first meal for the day. Remember, we had to do the Granddad ritual thing before anyone could eat, even after a long day at police headquarters.

The police thought it would be better to wait for Momma to get out of the hospital before pursuing matters any further, so I was picked up by the relatives, and the case was dropped temporarily.

Although there was nothing to do at Grandma's, it was crowded, I wasn't going to be taken to school, and I was mocked by the other kids who insisted that I had spent the day in jail, it was better than being pinned underneath Reverend Nasty another night.

After Momma was released from the hospital, she, Reverend Nasty, Grandma and I had an informal meeting at the station with the police to determine what would be done with Reverend Nasty.

Momma began. She talked and talked. I had never seen her so passionately convincing about anything before.

"He has treated her better than her own father!" Momma said, as she pulled from her purse an itemized list of all the things he had bought us. She continued, "That girl is a trouble-making liar who has been nothing but a problem her entire life!"

As Momma went on, I dropped my head and regretted ever telling a soul about what Reverend Nasty had done to me. Momma went on—proving, persuading and offering to bring documentation from the schools to verify my years of unruly behavior. The officers listened carefully as Momma's voice dominated the moment. Then before long, the meeting was over.

The police had decided there was not enough evidence to convict Reverend Nasty of anything at all. There would be no formal investigation, all charges were dismissed, and everyone was free to go.

The policewoman, who had typed the last time I was there, patted my back and told me as she escorted us out of the station, "Enjoy the gifts, allow your mother to be happy, and stop causing so much trouble. Can you do that?" I nodded, disconnected myself from feeling betrayed, pretended none of it ever happened and left with Momma and Reverend Nasty.

At home, I was alienated; it was them and me. Momma and Reverend Nasty would joke about, what they called, my "illusions" of *being* with him. Also, somehow he had convinced Momma that I was in competition with her for him. He told her that what really happened is that I had approached him, and when he wouldn't be with me, I lied about him to the police. He had gotten Momma to believe that I wasn't a child who needed protection, but that I was "the other woman"—an arch rival. He would tell Momma she was all the woman he needed and that he didn't want some skinny, little, ugly girl.

He began doing what he called "proving his love" to Momma by having sex with her in whatever room I was in at the time. I would immediately get out of there as fast as I could, but Reverend Nasty found a way to use that against me. He would tell Momma, "See, she only leaves because she can't stand to see you happy; I told you she wants me for herself."

Reverend Nasty continued to abuse me, but he wasn't the only one. I didn't bother telling anyone about the others. People weren't believing me anyway, so I gave up trying to be protected. I decided to suffer through it until I could protect myself. Besides, Momma said that if I continued saying that I was being molested, they were going to take me away. Maybe that's what Momma wanted them to do, but whether she knew it or not, she needed me.

I was always there to comfort her and call emergency after Reverend Nasty had beat her into a "crisis" followed by rape—his new favorite pastime since I had told everybody what he did to me. Without me, who would go around the house and collect the sponge rollers that he knocked out of her head when he slammed her around?

Just before starting high school, I found us a new place to live away from Reverend Nasty. But by this time, he had left Momma for good anyway. Now that he wasn't there to hit and fondle me anymore. Momma was beating me frequently and more brutally than ever before. And although we were in the same house, we had grown worlds apart.

During her hospital visits, I was staying with all kinds of different people in order to be close to school. I don't quite remember how we found many of the people I stayed with. I know that Momma met one lady in a candy store. But most of them were referred by a friend of a friend who knew someone who needed some extra money. Whatever the case, somehow I ended up with strangers. As a result, I witnessed my share of drug use, fights and crime.

I lived with people of different colors, professions and all kinds of beliefs. Changing Gods was often necessary to keep a place to live. If the family went to the Mosque, I was Muslim. If they went to Mass, I was Catholic. If they went to church on Saturday, I was Seventh Day Adventist. If they were Pentecostal, Apostolic or Church of God in Christ, I was "sanctified."

I was what I called a "fake-me-out" foster kid because I had no official paper work. I wasn't legitimately anything. I was an unclassified virtual orphan. I didn't belong to the system, I wasn't legally emancipated, I wasn't a ward of the court, a juvenile delinquent, adopted, or even a real runaway.

Having grown sick of living everywhere but home, I eventually convinced Momma that I could take care of myself when she was ill. I took care of the house and the German shepherd Reverend Nasty had given us. And I got myself off to school sometimes.

When there was no more food in the house, I took soda cans to the grocery store for a refund. Then I'd buy oatmeal, bread, bacon and dog food. I ate oatmeal, toast and bacon every day until the bacon ran out. Then there was just the oatmeal and toast until the bread ran out. Finally, I ate the oatmeal everyday and every meal until Momma came home.

After I shoveled a neighbor's snow, she invited me to her church, where I immediately became a regularly member. Momma would forbid me to tell the church people I needed food, so I took a job at a fast-food place, learned the city bus schedule and went to work to earn money for food.

The new church was different from the one Momma and I belonged to years before. There were no speaking opportunities, activities, choirs, picnics, retreats or chicken dinners in the fellowship hall. Sometimes there wasn't any heat or phone service either. It was a little pink building where five of the eleven members were the pastor's family. We could never attract and keep new members. It was as if the place had a revolving door. The pastor said people always left because they had worldly desires that they didn't want to give up. I thought people were leaving because there was no love in our church. We weren't drawing people with kindness. The talk and the feel of the place was always judgmental and condemning. *But what did I know?*

The doctrine was very restrictive. I could only wear dresses and skirts, no pants. Make-up and jewelry were forbidden, and I couldn't go anywhere. Everything was a sin and everybody was a sinner. I was allowed only to go to church and listen to gospel music.

The music part wasn't bad. Where the average sixteen-year-old with a house to themselves may have made some compromising choices, my wildest move was cranking up The Clark Sisters. And then there was my favorite singer—Vanessa Bell Armstrong! I knew every note of her albums, *Chosen* and *Peace Be Still*, by heart. I found such comfort in her extraordinary voice, and lip-syncing along with her helped me escape.

Although the church people, known as "saints," were teaching me to be terrified of God, Hell, the devil, dying, and the world in general, it was the only place I could try to belong.

At home, Momma began to be delusional and irrational. She heard voices and had hallucinations. She had also become radical with her rules and regulations. Mirrors were to be covered always so that people wouldn't see into the house. She also demanded that my shoes be pointed in the same direction. When they weren't, she accused me of practicing witchcraft. She also insisted that the neighbors were sneaking into the house through some secret tunnel in the basement.

"Them people puttin' sh-t in my food!" Momma would declare as she placed butcher knives in the window sills. Then she would yell out to neighbors sitting in their yards, "I'll kill you first!"

I didn't have a clue as to what was happening to Momma. Whatever was going on, I knew it wasn't going to end anytime soon. And I was scared.

The configuration of our house changed. Momma put the kitchen furniture in the dining room, removed all the curtains and replaced them with the bed sheets.

Life with Momma became more violent every day, and I wasn't sleeping well. It didn't help matters that after falling asleep—on the few occasions I was able to—I woke up to her standing over my bed looking crazed while brandishing a weapon!

After several months of this, I put a lock on my bedroom door and wired a phone line near the bed in case I ever needed to call for help. But Momma removed the lock and destroyed the phone jack completely.

I reached out to people in the best way I could, but I had a hard time convincing anyone that we needed help. Momma was good at acting reasonable in front of others. Once, to get proof of her strange behavior, I audiotaped her during one of her classic "wig out" moments. I gave it to my pastor and his wife. They took it, heard it and reprimanded me for violating Ephesians 6:1. That was the last of the cassette or any discussion about life at home for me.

Before long, Momma started locking me out of the house.

Winter or summer, it didn't matter. When I came home from school, work or church, I would find either the locks had been changed or my key had been taken off the ring. On these occasions, I'd go to a neighbor's—one she hadn't made angry—spend the night on the front porch, or go off into the night with strangers.

I would ride with anybody if they would take me.

Most of them were men who looked like trouble. They had guns, money and fast cars. They were shady looking characters—like something you would see on an eight-by-ten photograph hanging in the post office. Sometimes I got in cars packed with about four or five of them, but somehow I wasn't afraid.

Then there were the older men, the ones who looked like they would do what Reverend Nasty liked doing to young girls. But whether they were old or young, what they did once my life was completely in their hands always amazed me.

One man, Al was his name, drove me far away from home. I had no idea where we were going.

We ended up at some hotel. I was sixteen; Al was twenty-five.

Al left me in the car, checked us into a room, walked me to the door, kissed me on the forehead and left!

He left!!!

This happened all the time. Men I didn't know fed me, talked to me, seen to it that I was safe, then vanished! It was as though God had sent guardian angels. I could never reach them again; none of the phone numbers anyone ever gave me worked after they took off. And I never saw the same person twice.

When Al didn't come back for me, I called Theressa, who picked me up and took me home. Theressa was Grandma's neighbor, but more importantly, she was a member of my *role model buffet.*

There was a handful of people in this role model buffet—all positive individuals I admired without notifying them. They weren't rich or famous; they were just ordinary folks doing quality stuff. Our paths crossed from time to time. I rarely, if ever, spent time with any of them; I would just see them out and about in the community being sharp, intelligent and polished.

I called them role models and not mentors because they had little if any conscious participation in my life the way mentors do. These role models simply lived their own lives so powerfully that they inspired me from a distance. Then much like you do at a buffet, I would take from them and imitate qualities that I thought were good.

I was used to being locked out at night, but one night, while sitting outside, I began to grow uncontrollably angry with Momma, with the situation and with the whole difficult life I had been sentenced to living. In an instant, what had been my everyday routine suddenly struck me as absurd. And so I asked myself:

What the hell am I doing on the porch?

This had been an unusually rough day. I had walked to and from that broken down dump they were passing off as a high school. The walk each way was a hair shy of two miles, and never felt worth the effort. At work, I had been called stupid and made to clean the toilets because I was too nervous to count well at the register; and at church the pastor's wife said that I wasn't going to heaven.

Usually, I could tolerate Momma, but I wasn't up for her or anything else that night. I was tired, a little down and I felt worn. This time I refused to sleep outside like an animal! Momma had gone too far; everything had gone too far! It had all driven me into a rage, and in that moment I wasn't afraid of anything—least of all Momma! I was sick of Momma, and, as far as I was concerned, whatever was going to happen could happen. I was prepared for her to bring it on!

I rose from the cheap multi-colored lounge chair which Daddy had taken out of some dumpster way back when. With watery eyes, I threw the hat that matched the fast food uniform out into the street. Then in a single thrust and with all my might, I screamed as I broke into my mother's house. The noise was so loud that I scared myself. The front door split; wood went everywhere, and there she stood with her mouth open and her eyes stretched wide—silent.

After the initial shock of what I'd done, she began the cursing, the yelling, the threats. I had never said anything back to Momma when she went on like this, but this time my words preceded my thoughts, and I guess my logic was still on the city bus because I yelled back, I cursed back, I lost it right back at her! She charged towards me, and for the first time in my life, I didn't run.

I put my hands around my mother's throat, and I knew that there was no turning back now. Because if she ever made it over to that window she would stab me, without a doubt. And maybe I would let her—eventually. God knows I was tired. But she wasn't getting me without a fight.

I had decided that if the people ever came for us, they may have very well found my body with a knife sticking out of my skull but not before finding my crazy momma stomped into what would have been her very last "crisis!"

If the pastor's wife was right—if I was going to Hell—this night, I had made up in my mind that I wasn't going alone. Momma was going with me!

Somehow I did survive that night. Both Momma and I were spared, but for how long? I knew this was it for me; I had to go, and so I did.

Living and bouncing around started up again. I lived in almost twenty different places my last year of high school before realizing that I wasn't fitting in anywhere. It was always the same. The people didn't know how to love me in their homes, or I didn't know how to let them. Either way, I had no sense of security or stability. I had fallen through the cracks of society, and I didn't know how I got there. But that didn't matter now. I didn't have the luxury of contemplating my circumstances. Here was where I was, and there was only one thing to do: I had to save myself. So I left to live on the streets.

CHAPTER 3

Pulling the Pieces Together

Alone and disconnected from my place, my origin, my people and even myself, I still had to make it.

I'd run the full gamut of bureaucratic red tape, trying to get social service assistance, community outreach, non-profit organization support, or anything that would help me find a place in this world. Everywhere I turned I was told the same thing: "You're not a candidate for any of our programs."

I was always either too old, too young, too late, or only qualified as a teen mother. The drill was always the same: "I'm sorry we can't help you. Don't you have family? Are you being abused? Where's your father?" When I couldn't explain my predicament, I was sent away.

"Just go back home honey and try to work things out with your mother. You teenagers all think you have the answers. You just need to listen to your mother and let her help you through these growing pains. What you're feeling is normal at your age."

I left them, never understanding why no one understood.

I didn't know how to explain my life—any of it. I didn't know how to say that there was no place safe to go. I had a few relatives who were eager authoritarians, and I just didn't want to be in their homes.

"You may run a game on your poor sick mother, but with me, you have met your match!" they would boast. I intuitively knew that a tyrant bent on using me as a "tough love" rehabilitation project would have crushed my spirit, and I owed it to myself to preserve whatever enthusiasm for life I had left. More discipline was the last thing I needed.

I needed tenderness, something that had never been tried with me before. For once, I needed someone to guide me, protect me, validate my feelings and listen—not yell, not judge, not accuse, not punish, not beat, not criticize, not ignore—*just listen*.

I needed a mother, and, if not a healthy one, at least a sane one. I didn't have either. Momma had become insanity made manifest. I didn't know how I was supposed to sit down and have a reasonable conversation with a person who, by this time, was finger painting bloody moons, wearing the bed sheets and sprinkling Ajax on the floor to ward off demons.

I also didn't know how to address the "abuse question." Although my mother had physically hurt me, in our community, that was considered "normal" disciplining, and parents were entitled. It was the, "I brought you into this world; I will take you out" mentality.

I didn't know how to express that, while my mother had not broken any bones or burned me beyond recognition, I still felt abused.

I didn't know how to get anyone to understand that the abuse was in Momma's disapproving looks, the way she rolled her eyes as though the sight of me repulsed her, her magnification of my weaknesses and her failure to see my strengths, the humiliation that came with slapping me across the face in front of my classmates; the barking of my name, creating in me the fear of always being hit whether I was good or bad. Abuse was in the way that I was made to feel guilty or ashamed even when telling the truth, doing a completely selfless deed or just waking up on a new morning.

It was in the harsh way she dealt with me, handled me, responded to me. It was in the way she talked about me and closed ranks against me in front of people. It was in the way my mother bargained off my innocence in order to feel loved by a man who had abused me.

But I didn't *look* abused. So, I continuously begged for help with no success.

From what I could see, the only teens who were getting attention and support were into drugs, dropping out of school or becoming pregnant. I didn't fit into any of the categories. It was as though my problems weren't being validated because they hadn't driven me to drink.

The way I dealt with my life wasn't popular among other youth. The wildest things I had done was skip class to avoid being teased, leave church in the middle of a sermon to be on time for a Vanessa Bell Armstrong concert, and lie about being pregnant in order to get somebody to talk to me and be interested in my life.

By the way, that always backfired. Once they discovered I'd lied, my credibility was shot. I then found myself even more isolated.

The message was clear: no program or system was going to get me through this. I figured I had no other alternatives, so I started knocking on doors and asking strangers for help.

I went from one house to the other. Some people peeked out but didn't open their doors, while others thought it was a joke and laughed me off of the porch.

I took breaks periodically from my home-searching to use pay phones to call people, church folks, relatives—just somebody. I don't know what I thought anybody would or could do for me. I think I just wanted to talk; I was so alone.

When my collect calls were refused or not answered, I would resume my door-to-door crusade.

With night about to fall, I grew tired, and decided to come to terms with the possibility of having to finish my senior year of high school living in an alley.

Maybe it wouldn't be so bad, I thought. I could find a dry place, get a refrigerator box from an appliance store and buy some blankets from a thrift shop. I really believed I could make it work.

Fortunately for me, it never came to that. One of my classmate's mom found a homeless shelter in the basement of a sanctuary. The Baldwin Avenue United Methodist Church in Pontiac was kind enough to take me in against their policy. Minors weren't to be serviced without their parents.

It wasn't an awful arrangement. In fact, I found peace in knowing that I was done moving, running and searching.

The shelter wasn't festive, bright or decorative, but it was very clean and functional. The concrete floors were cold, and the eggshell colored walls displayed nothing more than a duty schedule for the staff.

A large brown woman with a flawless layered hair-cut began to show me around the place. This woman, Willie, was a self-appointed sergeant at arms. She didn't play, and that was clear from the start. With my classmate's mom now gone, I stood alone to receive the rules of the house and acquaint myself with strangers in what would now be my home.

Willie talked; I listened: "Bed time is 8:00 p.m. all seven nights, 'rise and shine' 7:00 a.m. all seven days. Lounging and sleeping aren't permitted. Any and all forms of relaxation are considered laziness and will not be tolerated. If you are not sick, you're expected to be up, dressed and prepared to go to work. If you don't have a job, yours is to look for one...oh that's right, you're in high school. Okay, well, doing something productive is always the name of the game, so school is fine.

"If you have nothing to do on the weekends, you are to

read a book or study. If you aren't reading, we assume you don't know how, and guess what? You are about to learn!"

"Visitors are welcome after dinner for one hour."

"Food is not allowed in the bedrooms at all, everyone is to eat together in the dining hall, and absolutely no food is permitted in from the outside.

"You don't have to attend church services upstairs, but you must remain quiet while they're happening."

The rules continued to effortlessly roll off Willie's lips. I followed her as she swiftly passed through the shelter, pointing out areas that I should become familiar with.

"Showers on the left, laundry on the right. Anything you want washed, put it here by Wednesday morning, and it will be ready for you within 24 hours—any questions?"

I didn't have any. That Willie was quite thorough. Strangely enough, I felt empowered and safe.

My room accommodated five cots and a crib. The shelter wasn't full when I arrived, so I had the room to myself until George and his mom came.

George was a seven-month-old bald baby with a smile that lit up the universe. He and his mother were hiding from his father. She was originally a white woman, but when I met them, she was mostly black and blue.

I adored George. I had two things to look forward to in my life at that time, George and the Tuesday clothing donations that shelter clients had first pick of for free. Once we made our selections, the public was allowed to buy the leftovers.

George's mom said that he must have known what time I came home from school because he would work his way to the side of the bed closest to the doorway and wait for me everyday. I'd rush in the door and down the hall, while tossing textbooks on the nearest cot, and make a beeline to his precious face with his perfectly shaped shiny head. I'd lift him out of the little jail crib thing where he'd been all day, and we'd play until dinner.

I watched dozens of people pass through the shelter. Some were recovering addicts, victims of house fires, domestic violence survivors, evicted tenants with children, or just people who felt dejected and hopeless. I made friends and just as quickly they moved on, but nothing was quite as disturbing as the day I rushed to George after school to find that without a good bye, he too had gone with his mother to retry life with his dad. I never saw George again.

Eventually, my enthusiasm became compromised. Willie was getting another job; Alice, the program director, was retiring; and I hadn't made any friends at the all-white high school I'd transferred to since moving to Pontiac alone. Still, I held on.

Sometimes people in the community came to the shelter, looking for someone who wanted to earn money doing odd jobs. I always volunteered; it was mostly yard work. The money came in handy. It was what I used to have the navy blue, silk, pleated dress, I got from the Tuesday donations dry cleaned for graduation day.

A few people from Detroit came to the commencement exercises. While I don't think any of them knew or cared where the blue dress came from or how I had struggled to get to that day, I was glad to see them there.

My relatives were very good at making appearances on special occasions and doing sporadic acts of kindness without participating in my real life. There were no feelings or emotional attachment to speak of, no consistency to rely on, and nurturing was out altogether, but I was always appreciative for whatever they could give whenever they could give it.

A major segment of my mission was over. I had graduated from high school by the skin of my teeth. Teachers and school counselors said it wouldn't happen, and if I were them, I may have believed it wouldn't happen either—considering my grades. But I wasn't them! I saw beyond my grade point average; I had vision for my life, and it was beginning to pay off!

Next, I desperately wanted to go to college, but I didn't know anything at all about how to do that. Then, one day, I received something interesting in the mail.

It was a colorful poster with a picture of a parachute on it from some private college up north. Nothing else was in the envelope—just the poster. That was enough for me. I liked the poster; besides, it was the only attention I had gotten from any college; that is, since Momma had scared off that one recruiter.

The school had spelled my name wrong, but it was close enough for me. In that moment, I decided, money or not, support team or not, acceptance letter or not, I was going to college! So, I bought a one-way Greyhound bus ticket, packed chicken wings in a shoe box, put all the money I had in my pocket and went to school.

I didn't know exactly where I was headed. In fact, I didn't know much about what I was embarking upon at all. I had a very poorly developed sense of fear, and I was ignorant to the odds against me. I was the first to go to college in my circle, so breaking through the ice headfirst and working my way to the other side was my only option.

Relatives came to the bus station to see me off, and I was very happy to see them, but as I was boarding, something strange happened.

Momma became distraught, started crying and sliding down a wall to the floor!

It was clear that she wasn't having a "crisis," so what was she having? What was she carrying on about?

We had been planets apart for years, and I hadn't lived with her for several months, by this time. I didn't think she even cared that I was leaving.

I certainly wasn't sad about going; I couldn't wait until

that bus pulled off.

An aunt ran over to console Momma. I was just looking at Momma. I wasn't buying the empty nest syndrome drama Momma was doing. I knew only two things: One, that bus was headed to a better life, and two, I was on it!

The frequent disregard for me and not receiving love throughout my life had thickened my skin––making me indifferent. I had stopped feeling. No one had shown an appreciation for me in all this time; I felt like they could keep it now. I decided that I didn't need love anymore; I needed a college degree.

The thirteen hour bus ride seemed endless, and when I arrived, I didn't know where to go. There I was in the middle of a Finnish rural community with everything I owned, and no place to put it.

"Are you here to go to school?" They asked.

"Yes, I am!"

"Then come on in; let's get you going."

I was on my way now!

The gentleman sat down at his computer terminal.

"What is your name?"

I got nervous. I knew my name wasn't in there, but I told him anyway. I thought, *Maybe we'd both be surprised!* Sure enough, he punched in my information, and there it wasn't!

He then turned to me, "When did you apply?"

That is when I came clean.

"I have to be honest with you. I don't think I did apply. There was a recruiter, maybe or maybe not from this school, who came to my house some time ago. My mother wouldn't cooperate with him, so the poor guy gave up.

"My mother has lost her mind, and if you know where my father is, tell me and we'll both know.

"My grades are poor, and even if I did, at some point, take the right college entrance test, I'm sure that I got all the wrong answers. I have no place to go, and I finished the only food I had coming here.

"I have eighty dollars in my pocket, and this poster your school sent me. I have looked at it every day while trying to earn enough money to get here. I have everything I own with me, and I want to go to this school.

"I am strong, hardworking and smart. I just don't have any of that in writing *yet*.

"I have heard kids here complaining all day about how they would rather be someplace else. This is the only place in the world that I want to be. Will it really hurt anything to let one person in your school who is pleading to be here, wanting to be here and needing to be here?

"If I don't perform well, kick me out, but please give me a chance. I will take this opportunity and make a life for myself. I promise. *Just please help me.*"

Although my voice never cracked, and my eyes always were in contact with his, the tears rolled.

The man left the room.

When he returned twenty minutes later, he brought people with him who were talking and moving fast all around me.

What were they doing?

Everybody had some kind of paperwork: applications, forms, letters...

I was overwhelmed with joy. They were letting me stay!

I was assigned my very own room in the brand new dormitory; it was the only thing available on such short notice. After all, I had showed up on the stairs of the school the very first day of classes, completely unprepared. But like a lot of other people, on that day, I became a full-time college student!

Angels continuously came into my life in the form of strangers. They were everywhere—in the financial aid office, in the admissions department and in the classrooms, but homelessness still plagued me to some degree.

While other students got regular mail, care packages and

visits from home, I contemplated places to go during semester breaks. Staying in the dorms wasn't school policy.

During breaks they chained and padlocked the doors for security reasons. After the dormitory was secured, no one could leave or enter.

Separate "on campus" housing was provided in another facility for those who had nowhere to go, but it was over and above standard room and board rates. With the earnings from my work-study job, I had just enough money to maintain myself during regular semesters.

One time I was unable to find a place to go for the week long spring break. So without telling anyone, I allowed them to lock me in the dorm. I bought food a few days before the dorms closed. On the day that the building was to be evacuated, I balled myself up and hid in a closet on the floor of my room until everyone was gone.

Now trapped inside the building, I held onto myself without moving or uttering a sound until I was certain the coast was clear.

That entire week, I lived like a fugitive. I had a systematic living plan. Lights were off at all times so that Campus Safety wouldn't get suspicious, and I disconnected the fire alarm when using my hot plate to cook.

At one point, I called Sherry, a friend who had stayed in the "on campus" housing, to let at least one person know that I was there. I had become afraid of the silence and of the dark.

The next day, Sherry brought me a bunch of candy. I pushed open the door as far as the chains would allow and gratefully received the bag of goodies. Her deed revitalized me, and I knew I was going to make it through.

Throughout the next few years, I encountered several stumbling blocks on my path, but I used them as stepping stones. Endurance had become an art form and by this time in my life, I had mastered it.

Initially, my grades were poor in college, but I was determined to excel, I learned to study and eventually became academically strong. With dedication and persistence, I transferred to a four-year university where my grades earned me a place on the Dean's List. I also came to understand how to be resourceful and financially savvy. With this knowledge, I rented an apartment, bought a mid-size, luxury sports sedan, and established myself as a solid citizen in the community.

Back at home, Momma was getting worse. She had fully developed a warped concept of reality and wasn't being treated for it.

Momma lived alone now and was being antagonized by her own thoughts. She was tormenting the neighbors and accusing them of raping their children, running prostitution rings, poisoning the dog, and trying to kill her. At least one of the voices she was listening to told her I was already dead.

Momma had started taking cabs to local funeral homes to pay respects to her only child. Some other voices were telling Momma I was alive but in danger and needed police protection. It was on these occasions that she would call Campus Safety or the County Sheriff or both in my college town, requesting that they conduct search parties for her missing child.

The first few times the officers came out around 3:00 a.m. to check on me, they were polite and concerned. After a few more visits, they were aggravated by the nonsense and questioned her motives. Finally, I was able to convince them of my mother's illness and with time, they spared themselves the trips.

The most frightening episode was when I got the call that Momma tried to shoot Grandma with a loaded gun! Fortunately, it didn't go off. The bright side of the incident was that, while it had taken almost ten years, everybody finally was agreeing that my mother needed help.

Relatives' interest in Momma and her problems were at an all-time high. Some of them had recently found God, and were involving themselves in her life. They were giving her fried okra, cutting the lawn, combing her hair, visiting with her and mailing her bills.

While I appreciated that Momma was finally getting the attention she needed—attention we both needed way back *before* she lost her mind—I didn't share the same attachment to my mother that everyone else seemed to have had.

I had long been drained from the years I suffered with Momma by myself, trying to find both of us the help we needed. Her issues were new to others but were a part of my past, and that is where I wanted to leave them. I had survived Momma, and I no longer had the energy to take myself back. I didn't feel obligated or guilty. I felt liberated and entitled to happiness. I was forgetting those things which were behind and reaching forward.

The relatives and their acquaintances didn't understand or appreciate my position on the matter.

I didn't drop my goals, give up my life and care for Momma like a daughter *should* have, they said. They said I didn't love my mother, so their disapproval became my punishment.

By this time, their rejection was a lot easier to shake. I was no longer a little girl who needed ice cream money or a ride to school. I was making a place for myself in a small corner of the world, and I believed in my future.

After receiving a bachelor's degree in Political Science, in preparation for law school, reality set in. Law had not been *my* dream; it was Daddy's. I decided not to go to law school; doing terrible on the LSAT (Law School Admissions Test) made that an even easier choice. Testing poorly turned out to be one of the best things that ever happened to me. Instead of law school, I enrolled full-time in graduate school.

While working on my master's degree, The reigning

Assistant Dean of Students suddenly left the position. They asked me to fill in until they got a permanent replacement! While the position was only temporary, I saw it as a grand opportunity to eventually become a polished professional. I had my own office, complete with staff and a secretary—how cool! I was on my way.

Even though I experienced my share of ups and downs as a higher education executive, I continued to throw myself into the industry by working, studying, and becoming familiar with all the particulars of the profession. I immersed myself in my work. The goal was to become president of a university by my early thirties. And I was headed in the right direction. As I grew more knowledgeable, I began obtaining solid positions as an instructor, a facilitator, a director, a leader...all in step with the plan. I was right on time and on track. But something happened that I hadn't planned for.

As I was plowing along the path, I didn't find my higher education journey to be the challenging, fulfilling or economically rewarding adventure that I thought it would be. And while I had managed to preserve a great portion of my enthusiasm for life, something was still missing from it.

At work, my sick time, personal days, and vacation time were depleting fast. I always found reasons not to go in.

I just didn't want to be there.

And like most Americans, I was living paycheck to paycheck, with less than one-thousand dollars saved and overwhelming credit card debt.

I had forty more years before I could retire, and I wasn't going to make it!

What in the world was I going to do?

I had become enslaved to material things, and I didn't own any of them. They owned me. And boy did I have bills! Increasing my professional responsibilities, working second jobs, and participating in get-rich-quick programs had all taken me down dead-end streets, and did I mention to you

73

that I had bills! Anyway, I was getting by, sure, and my life wasn't miserable, but it wasn't one of heel-kicking bliss either. I wanted to be absolutely delighted with life, and I wasn't.

I thought, maybe the secret was in owning my own business. So, I rolled up my hunter-green oriental rug; sent back the designer water; scooted the five caster button-tuft chair to the car; stripped the wallpaper, and loaded the microwave, mini-fridge and stereo sound system into the trunk. Then off I went into the world with no plan and no start-up capital.

Bills mounted and lean days were many, but determined to be my own boss, I secured the resources to buy a novelty print shop franchise for which I had no passion. I hated being there more than anything else I'd ever done, so I closed the business and halted my spinning wheels.

My God, what in the world was I doing? What had I done so wrong?

I had gotten degreed up and followed all the "rules" for being successful in our society. Why then wasn't anything flourishing in my life?

Ironically, I was still hopeful and fastened with faith, so I did the only thing left to do. I became silent.

There comes a time when, after having tried all the doors, being quiet is the only one open. I had associated silence with punishment for so many years, that doing it for the sake of growth had not occurred to me. Now it was time to try it.

I had been moving too much, conversing too much and looking aggressively for the answer. The truth is, the answer was always inside of me. I had always known what I needed to know to live a good life, but for some reason we don't always trust ourselves. We look to others to define us even when we think we are making independent choices. But many times our decisions are still derived from some kind of societal expectation. I had been trying for so many years to fit in and look like success that I completely disregarded my intuition, my voice, my uniqueness, my God given wisdom.

Clarity had been waiting for me to let it get a word in all this time and I never did...until now.

My stillness revealed that while I'd always had charisma, drive, and stamina, my soul was scarred along the way. This scarring caused me to play small in life. I'd chased the icons of success and appeared to have been winning, but not so. In my efforts to be accepted and loved, I had allowed myself to be distorted. The mask I was wearing for the world had become so thick that it was now hiding me from myself. I didn't know what I wanted. I was just trying to obtain what I thought you were supposed to want. I was trying to look like I had it all together without fully embracing the essence of my being. Ambition had allowed me to win on some levels, but not the ones that mattered most. I needed to heal so that I could reclaim my courage to live as tall and as large as God could imagine for my life.

When I realized that I was not who I wanted or needed to be, I decided to restore my personal integrity. I decided to become honest about my value and committed to regaining my own sense of truth. I decided to sit my self down somewhere and hear God. This is when the healing began. And my life was made over.

The Power of Awareness

This new quest was born out of my desire to know myself and express that fully. So there is where I started. I wanted to feel so that I could heal, and I wasn't going to constrict myself anymore. I mattered enough to myself to investigate the real truth about who I was.

I warmed up to myself, slowed down the pace and gently tracked the emotional beats along my rugged path.

I began reflecting on my most memorable and uncomfortable childhood experiences. It was then I realized that beneath the numbness had been years of anger.

I continued to sit with myself, and I refused to be ashamed of any of my feelings; I had been without them too long. Without censoring or judging my opinions, I found the courage to be ruthlessly honest about why I was angry, very angry. And so I took the time to vent to myself.

I was angry that my parents hadn't been more responsible for the life they brought into the world. The Humane Society wouldn't have given these people a puppy! Who did they think they were subjecting me to their already messed up lives? Why weren't they screened? You even need a license to fish, but anybody with working genitals can be given the awesome assignment of bringing forth human life. Why would you have a child when you know you're checking out of the world soon? Why would you pick a fast talking, womanizing bum, with no income, to father your child? Why would anyone "knock up" a dying woman then take off?

He claimed he left because he never felt appreciated or respected by her family. He said they didn't like him. He said they wouldn't loan him money to marry her. He said the Provider was the reason he lost some big real estate job way back when—of course this traumatized his entire life and locked him out of success forever.

He said they all teased him about eating rice out of pots, and spitting it through the gap of his teeth while talking junk in front of Granddad's TV. He said they did all this; yet he had no problem leaving me, his flesh and blood, to be cared for by his "enemies."

Yes, I was angry!

I was angry because my life had been one big demonstration of abandonment. Being passed on, passed over and passed up was the rule, not the exception. No one would claim me as their own, advocate for me, stand in the gap for my feelings, nurture my wounds or protect me from new ones. I was indeed angry, and I could feel! I could even feel what I believed people had been saying back then, instead of helping me.

I felt that white people were saying: "Well, there is so much out there now for colored children in the ghetto. I pay my taxes and donate to charities all the time. Can't *you* people do something for yourselves?"

Black people then replied: "Y'all the ones with the money and the power, and ain't none of them programs what they cracked up to be. We don't think nothing's wrong over there anyway. That girl looks okay to us. She just bad and need to be 'whupped.' What we suppose to do anyway? We couldn't do nothing for nobody if we wanted to with whatchu payin'. We got enough on us just trying to deal with our own kids as we're barely making ends meet. How are we suppose to take on somebody else's headache. Look like the teachers or the schools would do something? That's what they are paid for."

Once the school got wind of this, it felt as though their take was:

"What are we supposed to do? We get no support from parents. They have quit raising their children and left it all up to the educators. They think we're professional babysitters. Many of these kids suffer hardships that just aren't our responsibility. We have enough to worry about, trying not to get shot by these emotionally disturbed brats that many parents send to school hungry and unprepared. If a child is being neglected at home, then there's where the problem needs to be rectified. We give homework and follow the lesson plans; that's it! We can't be their parents and psychologists too. We aren't paid enough as it is to be teachers! This girl is probably lying just to get attention anyway. She is and has always been a behavior problem. All we can do is have the school counselor call the police. After that, it's up to them to deal with."

The buzz of the cops felt like:

"This child doesn't appear to have the characteristics of an abused child. She isn't withdrawn or distraught. In fact, she is exceptionally bright, level-headed and looks nothing at all like a victim. She's not frightened or anxious. Look, she isn't even crying. The mother says she's making it up to get attention. Since the child has a strong demeanor, the mother is probably right. "There's no need to investigate this any further. We met some of her family members, and everyone seemed sane enough. They dressed well, and mentioned God. So from this, even though we didn't do any looking, it is our finding as competent law enforcers that the girl has a wild imagination. We are sending her back home to live with the mother, her people and the Reverend Child Molester. Go home little girl and be good. Case closed. Shred the report and let's get some donuts!"

Back with the relatives, the tone of the conversation felt like: "I told you she was gonna be just like her daddy. Now she's back in our faces. Why should we have to take care of her? They thought she was too good for us when she was a baby, now they got the nerve to need somebody! Well, we already raised our own kids and some of their kids too. We already spared one of these grandkids from being put up for adoption and another one was even on our health insurance. We ain't doing no more. We did our part for our own. Let the police find her no-good-for-nothing daddy and make him be a man for a change?"

Then there was Daddy.

During one of his on-the-move, foot-out-the-door, gotta-go, express talks, it felt like he was always saying: "I'm not able right now, baby. Daddy's had a run of bad luck. Whatever I've had though, I've always shared with you. The trouble is, I never had anything, but I got some deals in the lay-a-way. Yeah, I'm working on something big and when it comes through, I'll get with you. I will; daddy promise!

"But you know, back when I was trying to do for you when you were small, your Granddad and those people would down me and poison your mother and everybody against me, so I couldn't do what I wanted to. They always stopped me.

"Now that I have taken the low road and bailed out, I don't know what to tell you. I always pray for you though—between the births of my other kids. I can't really take care of them the way I want to either, but I pray for all of you everywhere. I ask God to look down on you wherever you are and bless you. Maybe the church can help you, sweetheart, because I can't."

Then I could hear the church folk:

"Thank you, Jesus, hallelujah, praise the Lord, little sister! Nobody loves you because God is punishing you for being evil. Fall down on your knees and beg Him to forgive you for wearing pants, before it's too late.

"What do you mean you need help? What are you talking about your mother doesn't always remember who you are?

"You don't have any more oatmeal in your house because you need to be fasting for forty days and forty nights! What do you mean you're afraid of what's happening at home? You need to be afraid of Hell because that's where you're spending eternity if you don't stop wearing earrings. And hell is a lot hotter than that pressing comb your mother throws at you!"

So there I stood without remedy or recourse. Everybody seemed to believe I was somebody else's responsibility, leaving me to be no one's at all. I knew I was angry about that, but I didn't know why. Why did it matter that I'd been deserted? Asking this question unveiled another emotion. Pain.

Beneath all of the anger had been pain. I hurt. I felt a deep agonizing emptiness that I hadn't felt before. I hurt because I was worth loving, but as a child I hadn't found anyone who agreed with me. I hurt because hurting was overdue. I hurt because nothing else was available after the anger. The entire experience of peeling back the layers of my emotions was not easy, but it was working. I hurt, and I hurt until I became afraid. So that was it.

At the bottom of it all, there was fear. I was afraid. I was afraid that my birth would never be good news to anyone but me. No one had celebrated my existence in a consistent and meaningful way. My fear was that no one ever would.

Now exposed and vulnerable, I cried. I cried about all of it. I cried about what I knew, and what I didn't. I cried just because I was crying. Eventually, my tears brought about a freedom that would be permanent and complete. I had cried so much that I became liberated, and with this new liberty, I was renewed. It was this moment of cleansing that the answer to my riddle, proceeding the first chapter of this book, became plain:

Riddle:
If it takes a village to raise a child,
what is a child to do when the village is asleep?

Answer:
Be grateful for what had always been God's protection,
pardon the sleepyheads of the past,
and live powerful enough to help wake the village for others.

This had marked the beginning of my breakthrough, and ultimately my success. Once I made up my mind to truly let go of the baggage, *how* to let it go became clear. The answers were distinct. I would have to change my perspective about people in order to become whole, and I was up for it. I had found the courage to forgive.

Being newly authentic meant not needing permission, validation or acceptance anymore. It meant that while I could respect that some felt entitled to have opinions about my work, my life, my choices...I ultimately only needed to acknowledge, please, and answer to One.

After pulling the pieces together, I was able to recognize how emotional baggage blocks spiritual, physical, and financial success. It affects how we live, earn, believe and choose absolutely everything in our lives!

My self-discovery process continued and in fact, became more profound, more intense. I found the courage to challenge every notion and element of knowledge that had been imposed on me by the world.

Because of my lack of fulfillment at work and my failure to make things better with entrepreneurship, I was particularly interested in the concept of *retirement.* The meaning of retirement was one of many nonsense notions that society had defined for me—for all of us. It seemed to me that the idea of retirement, as we were taught, meant that you work to pay bills for the bulk of your life, while postponing all the things you *truly* want to do until your winter years. I didn't want to do that, and I don't believe anyone else does either. Examining this perception would be the revolution I needed not only to gain control of my own life but also to help others do the same! I believe we all know that the traditional notions of retirement are illogical and not much to look forward to; but we just didn't know what to do about it...until now.

The first thing we have to do is look at what we've bought into all this time. There are three major myths that have helped to prevent the freedom and wealth that you could have otherwise been enjoying.

Myth #1 - Retirement Comes During the Last Part of Life

Why do we have the common belief that life has to be compartmentalized?

We have been socially manipulated into thinking that labor and leisure are separate events that happen at different stages of our lives. And so we have chopped life into three pieces.

The first piece of life is set aside for school. We are told to learn a skill, a trade, something. Then, when that is finished, the second part begins. We are to take that acquired schooling and go to work in whatever field we learned. Take no thought to what we love, what our real interests are or where we feel most capable. Just work for forty years, forty hours a week without question. Meanwhile as we labor, we secretly wish that we had the money to actually go somewhere with the vacation time our supervisor may or may not approve. As we long for some small oasis of freedom, we try to squeeze happiness in on the weekends, between errands, laundry or commitments that have nothing to do with advancing our own lives.

Finally, there is the third piece of life — the grand finale we've all been waiting to have for sixty-five years. *(Drum roll here)* Retirement! They have hyped us up about crossing this imaginary finish line ever since our very first day of work.

I remember thinking if I worked really hard they'll acknowledge my value by giving me a plaque, a fancy watch, a co-worker comedy roast, a big cake with buttercream icing, and a nice pension that I must use sparingly so that I don't outlive the money. Oh, how I thought I would enjoy the great adventures of discount coffee at fast food restaurants, sturdy walking shoes, 24-hour television shopping networks, and senior citizen trips on chartered buses.

They have convinced us that in this final piece of life, we *should* be satisfied with unlimited fishing, golfing, gardening, and regular doctor visits. By the way, this is our destiny if and only if, we save properly and avoid illness so that we have both the cash and the strength to live this "great" life.

I didn't want it.

I didn't want to spend two-thirds of my life trying to earn the privilege of becoming free one day. I wanted to be free *today*. So, I revolutionized the meaning of retirement in my life. I decided it meant something different, something promising, something hopeful, and something to partake of right now!

I integrated enjoyment and work into the overall meaning of my life! That in and of itself gave me a new freedom that made sense. I was then ready to do my life's work. *What!? Work! But I thought retirement means that you don't work.*

This question leads us to the second myth about retirement.

Myth #2 - Retirement Means You Don't Work

We have been sold an image of retirement that means not working. This too is a delusional premise that limits us. Retirement does not mean that you don't work. The truth is, we need to work. It helps us stay involved in the circulation of life; it keeps us healthy and spirited. We must do *something* with ourselves. Retirement, as we have known it, means that we do nothing all day, everyday until we die. But doing *nothing* diminishes and eventually cuts us off from vitality.

Retirement, the way it is currently set up, isn't natural. Living a life that lacks purpose, direction and aim runs contrary to what it means to be human. Permanent rest and relaxation are damaging in every aspect of life. Human beings were engineered to be useful and challenged. Our bodies and brains were designed to move, work, and serve. It is how we contribute and devote our lives that helps us identify ourselves. Without *occupation* of some kind, we lose the central organizing principle of our lives. And this jeopardizes our entire motive to live.

There are some cultures where our prevalent notion of retirement doesn't even exist. They don't have a word for sitting the elderly down and counting them out of being a vital part of society. As a result, their elders are physically and physiologically healthier, experience less depression and live much longer than the seniors of our culture.

Retirement, as it currently stands, is a societal concept of defeat. Humankind, in its own arrogance, has dismissed the usefulness of older people, and in the brainwashing of it all, older people, often dismiss themselves from life.

What I am suggesting is that it is not our place to withhold our time, energy and talents regardless of age; nor is it our place to tell anyone else to. Your work will always be needed by evidence of your very existence. In other words, if you're still breathing, there is something left for you to do. What's more, we actually want it this way!

We want to be useful. We want to be constructive. We want to feel worthwhile. We are only preoccupied in our society with quitting our jobs because either we hate our work, somebody at our work, or we simply want to do something else more enjoyable. But still, we want to work!

We might want to slow down some or change our venue a bit, but still, it seems, people want to work. Even after a much needed vacation, we always want to return to some meaningful work that will give our lives the balance needed to call ourselves *complete.*

Consider the many people who have taken advantage of full-time, part-time or volunteer work opportunities after "retiring" from a job of twenty plus years. Have you ever wondered why they go back out there? The money may be one reason. But it's also because we intuitively know that there is something more than a paycheck inside of working. Working brings about fulfillment, and the truest experience of fulfillment comes from living our passion. The only problem is, some people don't know what their passion is. If that is you, not to worry, we will talk about that later.

For now, know that not only do we need and want to work, it is our duty to work. Retirement isn't about having it made in the shade with lemonade on white sandy beaches, twenty-four hours a day for twenty years. Retirement isn't living a reckless life of fun-filled frolic.

Retirement is taking on the responsibility as a brilliant life form to make a contribution with your gifts. It is your life's contribution that will pay for the space you take up on earth.

Retirement is the freedom to design the life you've always wanted as a gesture of gratitude for having a life at all.

Retirement is when you move into your own sense of fullness and purpose. It is doing something that imprints your time here and says that you didn't wait for any certain age to live meaningfully.

I stake my claim to retirement today because I retired *from* self-defeating thought forms that have long stopped working for many of us, and I am absolutely free to live the life of my dreams now, today and everyday!

Speaking and traveling all over the world, designing success resources and finding new ways to help people maximize their potential is simply a natural extension of my personality. It is my passion, and I absolutely love what I do. It is a manifestation and expression of my truest joy, and I can't imagine life without it.

I retired by comprehensively pursuing happiness with my whole life. This means that I have incorporated and planned everything—spiritually, emotionally, physically and financially—from a holistic perspective. This outlook has brought me tremendous freedom, and it's just a bonus that it brings wealth. Why would I ever want to quit *working*?

Myth #3 - Retirement Means Sudden Wealth

A lot of people think that retirement is an economical thing—a matter of finance. And in part, it is, but money is just one element of the total package required to live a good life.

Not a day goes by that someone doesn't ask me, "So how did you make your money...what line of work were you in that caused you to retire?"

This question demonstrates a prime example of our need to change our thinking and elevate our understanding about success in general. Why do we naturally associate early "retirement" with some kind of financial windfall? The truth is, what I "did" to make money continues to be what I do to make money. Why do we speak of it in past tense?

Somehow we believe that our only hope for escape from lives we hate is to get rich *first*. Then and only then can we do what we really want to do. It is the very nature of this thinking that defeats us.

Doing what you really want to do with your life simply requires *doing* what you really want to do with your life! You don't have to pay for the privilege with a wad of cash up front. Money isn't the cure all for a miserable life. Money is a fringe benefit that comes *after* you improve the life you already have.

Why then do so many make the assumption, upon reading the title of this book, that all in one sitting I landed a golden goose that lays golden eggs? What is wrong with earning money while enjoying and loving your whole life at the exact same time? That brings me to another point.

Since when does the old retirement mean big money anyway? After all, we all know at least one somebody who has worked their entire life, have since traditionally retired and now can't make ends meet. It doesn't make a lot of sense when you look at it closely from all angles does it? What it boils down to is that we really have a crippling concept that makes people scared to get old. So, why do we have to gauge our happiness according to timelines set by someone else? The fact is, we don't. You don't.

You can begin today creating new truths for yourself that will empower your life.

We are the same age that we were yesterday, everyday, even on our birthday. Have you ever noticed that when people ask you, "How does it feel to be another year older?" we never know how to answer them? That is because it really feels no different. It is simply another day. And if we continue to work on ourselves, develop ourselves and grow on a daily basis, we actually have more to give, not less. So in the larger scheme of things, what does getting older have to do with anything?

Now you must ask yourself, "What is possible for my life if I change the way I have it all set up in my mind, if I change my beliefs about being too old, too young, too anything?" What if you started to question every disempowering belief that has governed your life?

What if you believed that it is never too late to start again? What if you somehow found ways to see being a single parent as an advantage? What if you stopped seeing yourself as someone who is on a fixed income or a limited budget? What if you believed that there was no glass ceiling in corporate America? What if you believed that your heart had never been broken? What if you believed that you could never get sick? What if you believed that everyone at work wanted to see you succeed? What if?

You can always go back to the old beliefs tomorrow. For some people, the notion of struggle and impossibility will always be there. Helplessness will remain available as an option for those who choose to have it. But for now, you have absolutely nothing to lose by pretending that nothing is in your way. What if you believed that anything was possible for you regardless of your present circumstances? And if you believed all of this right now, what could become of your life?

After fully understanding the principles of this process you should be confident that you will always have an income. This is why:

When you follow your passion in life, you have the **ABC's** of financial security—*Always Being Compensated*. You never stop earning when you do what you love. Money is bountiful, and you will always have it. Throughout the years, how you express your passion will no doubt vary and take on different forms. But these natural changes won't hinder you because when you consistently evolve, refine and reinvent your God given work, it will always have shelf life.

When your level of commitment, responsibility and involvement goes beyond the idea of just earning money, it shows. You also tend to be the best at what you do, and when you are the best, you can't be denied. Ultimately, your needs will always be met in abundance.

While being rich is not required to be truly retired or happy, it's very likely that you will become wealthy practicing the principles in this book. Many people have emailed us with reports that they already have. Being financially rich is a choice. If you choose to be wealthy, please know that your goal is very realistic in this wonderful land of opportunity, but character growth comes first. Then, the money follows—not the other way around. You have to allow yourself to have new beliefs in order to create new opportunities, options and possibilities for your life. This is what it takes to attract wealth.

The foundation of my message is simply this:

By dumping emotional dead weight, unlearning self-defeating beliefs, and discovering your passion, you will position yourself for a life beyond what you may have never imagined. You *CAN* live an extraordinary life right now and always!

Within these pages, as an obedient servant of God, I submit my understandings, experiences and perspectives for the edification of your magnificence. I am honored and I thank you for the opportunity you have given me. In the previous chapters, I shared my life with you to demonstrate a minute example of what's possible. I hope that you have been inspired and are ready to move forward. The rest of this book is designed to help unleash YOUR potential. This is my way of saying to you: enough about me my friend, it's your turn!

CHAPTER 4

The Most Critical Investment You Must Make Right Now!

Do you have a belief system that corresponds with having plenty? Are you standing with a door wide open for prosperity—eating, sleeping, thinking and moving inside of abundance? Or are you hating your job, attracting nut cases that resemble love, and spending every check before it is earned? If your situation is the latter, this is the result of an impoverished mentality, and something will need to change in order for you to be truly successful. Ask yourself, "What is in my energy and demeanor that tells the world that I'm available for mediocrity, nonsense, abuse, neglect or drama?"

You don't want to be like the average person who says they want a better life, but they are projecting something different.

Some believe that the only opportunity they'll have to live their dreams will have to come courtesy of some unpredictable windfall—a lawsuit, a turned over Armour truck in the road, a rich honey, a donation from Bill Gates, something, anything!

They don't realize they can be financially self-made should they disregard all the negative messages they have received through the years and recognize their true value. Surely, if all you have ever heard was "you can't, you shouldn't, wealth is a long shot, that won't work, and you won't make it" this is what you will believe.

Many people have bought the bill of goods that say your best chance at success is to stand in the lottery line and try to buy their dream for a dollar.

For some, lady luck might come, but why wait for her to decide what she wants to do? It's much safer to purposely navigate your own course of life rather than passively leaving each moment to chance. With you in control, your prosperity is guaranteed!

Success Isn't Hard

Being successful is not as difficult as it's made out to be. There is an arrangement form to success, and there will be absolutely nothing you can't have if you apply certain principles to your life. But before beginning to apply these principles, you must make a decision.

I mean really make an intentional, planned and calculated *decision* to raise your standards. You have to make a deliberate appointment with success or you'll never meet it. You must decide.

As we all know, prosperity isn't something that arrives in the mail. We have to be conscious of our quest. To *decide* is to conclude that nothing else is an option. If there ever was anything else to select, it now no longer exists, because you've cut it off.

Most people haven't achieved simply because they

haven't decided to. Instead of improving their lives on purpose, they wait passively for something good to happen to them. They wouldn't mind living better if it doesn't put them out of their way or take too long, and they wouldn't mind being successful if other people would just support them. Average people are usually willing to take a few knocks, but challenges eventually scare them off. Simply put, they lack persistence.

At the first sight of an obstacle, average people surrender to the jaws of defeat. "If it ain't one thing, it's another," they say. You will find them complaining about who didn't help and what didn't happen. Finally, full of disappointment and regret, they eventually stop trying. However, when you have *decided,* there can be no other way for you but success; so take the time to gird yourself with the built-in drive that makes it impossible to give up.

Once you have *decided,* the next thing to do is understand that whatever you've accumulated in life has been a direct consequence of your mindset. The friends and acquaintances you have, the work you do, where you live, what you drive, where you go, who and what you've attracted into your life ––it has all been acquired based on your thinking composition. Every aspect of your world is somehow a result of your own creation.

Each One of Us has Authored Whatever Life We are Now Living

Until you deliberately rewrite it, your book will always be the same. If it is your finances you are unhappy with, something within your belief system has helped to create lack in your life. Money will not be plentiful if the mindset is destitute. So the mentality is the first place your work must begin.

The money doesn't usually come before the freedom in this success plan. You have to initiate your road to freedom first. Where the pieces of your life come together, there will be liberty; and with having a new sense of control over the emotions that can suppress us, the money comes.

As we've discussed, *retirement* doesn't mean you just go and pick up a big check and buy away all your heartache; you must first do the mental and emotional preparation that elevates your mindset to even know where the check is!
If by chance you already have financial wealth, but you aren't happy, the strategies in this book will work to help you unleash fulfillment for yourself. Having said this, the greatest investment for anyone to make immediately is not in the hottest annuity, blue chip or dividend reinvestment program.

Your most critical investment to make right now is in your personal growth and development—the act of expanding your awareness!

According to Will Henry,"An open mind collects more riches than an open purse." Before you can experience money beyond what you currently have in your life, you'll have to refurbish your understanding. We are transformed by the renewing of our minds, and transformation is the key to unlocking the first door to prosperity.

Renew Your Mind

Develop a wealth building attitude. Obtain an appetite for excellence. Desire to be progressive, evolved, enlightened. It is these things that determine your prosperity status. Remember, all things are created twice: first, internally (in our minds) then externally where the world can see. But the mind is where it starts. What you obtain financially is always going to be in direct proportion with your thoughts, beliefs and imagination. So we must first acquire an "abundance attracting" mindset. Without it, money will have a difficult time finding its way to us. If by chance it does reach our lives, if the belief system doesn't meet the criteria for maintaining the newly found wealth, the money won't last.

How many times have you seen news reports of lottery winners who hit for millions, only to go broke a few years later? Often, people think losing fast money is normal. "Easy come, easy go," they say. They assume the the golden pot must have been carelessly overspent, but I guarantee the loss was about something much deeper. If you're internally impoverished, your money will match.

Learn Something Different

When you think differently, you obtain different results. So you must make it a conscious and deliberate priority to become improved. Real retirement is to be free. Freedom can't happen without becoming new. Reinventing yourself is the core of your first investment. It's the act of being reborn to a new state of consciousness. It's the willingness to give up justifying why things didn't, don't and won't work for you. I am talking about replacing the very seed of your belief system with one that will have you instinctively making better choices.

Happiness can become your routine. You no longer have to work hard for poor results that leave you dissatisfied and drained. Rather than get frustrated, ask yourself, "Why have I done it this way for so long?" While pondering this, consider your beliefs, your talk and your focus from day to day. How do you usually respond to life?

What are your thoughts? What are your opinions about yourself and others? How do you perceive daily encounters and experiences? Is your general approach to living upbeat and hopeful? Or are you just getting life done? Whatever your method of operation, it's a result of how your mind has been shaped, and this is what has formed your whole life. Your belief system has guided every choice, decision, companion selection, employment opportunity and everything else you have ever known. It has been the source of all your motivations. If your belief system has not molded the life you desire, how you think will need to change. Using the same outlook that created the life you have will not be effective for designing a better future.

Without inner restructuring, improvement will be marginal, if at all. To make significant positive changes in your life, you will need to decode your emotional DNA, so to speak. We know that DNA is the genetic code that determines your physical make-up. It decides your hair and eye color, height, skin tone, and such. What I mean by emotional DNA is the information you have allowed to influence your thinking throughout the years. This is your emotional make-up, and it has prescribed the way you do everything in life. It's your emotional DNA that determines your values, goals and beliefs. The question is, does your emotional coding help you make healthy choices that render favorable outcomes, or does it yield pain?

Most People Don't have Wealth Building Attitudes

They don't look beyond what's apparent to the naked eye. They say, "I'll believe it when I see it!" but it doesn't work that way; there is no faith in that statement. Anybody

How I Retired at 26!™

A step-by-step guide
to assessing your freedom
and wealth at any age.

Asha Tyson

ATD Publishing

ATD Publishing

---

*This book, these efforts, my life is dedicated to
The Almighty, my Refuge:*

*I am everything I am
because You loved me.
When everyone had forsaken me
You took me up.*

*If it takes a village
to raise a child,
what is a child to do when
the village is asleep?*

— Asha Tyson

Contents

Chapter 1
When Born to Win, but Left to Lose
(Part I)

Chapter 2
When Born to Win, but Left to Lose
(Part 2)

Chapter 3
Pulling the Pieces Together

Chapter 4
The Most Critical Investment
You Must Make Right Now!

Chapter 5
How to Deal with Difficult People

Chapter 6
How to Cope with Difficult Circumstances

Chapter 7
Escaping the Hidden Traps that
Can Make & Keep You Broke

Chapter 8
How and Where to Find Your Wealth

Chapter 9
Discovering the #1 Ingredient to Success

Chapter 10
Money

FOREWORD

You have the power within you to make your life whatever you desire. As the saying goes, "It's easier said than done." However, Asha Tyson has written this book to give you practical steps on how to do just that. If you are not already, think for a moment how it would feel, going through life pursuing your passion rather than a pension. Recent studies indicate that 87% of Americans go to jobs every day that they hate. This book will serve as a tool to teach you how to live a life of adventure, meaning and joy. It might sound far fetched, but the author has done it, and has devoted her life to traveling around the world, writing, speaking and teaching others how they can do the same with their lives.

Creating a life that gives you what you really want might not seem doable because of your present situation or circumstance, but it can happen, if you're willing to make the commitment, invest the time and do whatever is required. Asha has written this book from her first hand experience, lays the process down, and makes it possible for all of us to empower ourselves, to transform our lives, and to show up for ourselves 100%.

If you are willing to embrace the challenges of life, live your truth and courageously bring your talents and gifts to the fore front, you will accomplish things that will amaze others and surprise you. This book is insightful, thought provoking and life altering. Asha is not only dynamic and inspirational, but she is beautiful inside and out, and will ignite a sense of urgency and activate in you your power to choose to retire from what you're doing if it's not your heart's desire, take control of your future, and live a rewarding life right now.

One of my favorite quotes is: "Life is God's gift to us, and how we live our lives is our gift to God." Asha is challenging all of us to live a gifted life that we can all be proud of. Congratulations Asha, you've done yourself proud!

Les Brown
Best-selling author
Live Your Dreams! & *It's Not Over Until You Win*

A Personal Letter from Asha Tyson...

Dear Winner,

     I'll tell you right out of the gate, this book is not for people looking for a "get-rich-quick" scheme. It's a tool for those who are serious about building and maintaining financial wealth that lasts. I further suggest, it is not for those who are not ready to change unsuccessful habits. Surprisingly, some people subconsciously like struggle. If they couldn't complain, what in the world would they talk about?

     If you are still reading, I believe you are the person who is ready to embark upon a wonderful journey of fulfillment. And I give you applause! You have found a companion guide to creating a life of freedom and wealth. Think of it as having a one-on-one conversation with a successful friend who really wants to see you have the life you desire. And if you'll let me, I'd be honored to help you. Here, I'm offering what I used to realize my own dreams. This success formula has changed many lives and will continue to for millions of others.

     <u>How I retired at 26!</u> serves to bring you a solid condition of passion and power over your life that profit

alone can't do. "Retirement" isn't solely an economical event, it encompasses the theory of "complete package" living. I did want material wealth, but I also wanted to be fearless, have healthier relationships, and live at my spiritual, emotional, and physical best. This book teaches you how to do that for yourself. Acquiring only the financial part is like settling for a map—just a symbolism of the land itself. But in this book, we will be possessing the actual territory!

During our time together in the first three chapters, I share very personal experiences about myself, including the early accounts of neglect, abuse and homelessness. I pray it inspires you to realize a higher level of potential for yourself.

Regardless of who you are, where you're from, what mistakes you've made, how much or little you have, who said you couldn't, who said you shouldn't, what school you attended, what school you didn't attend, where you work, if you work or how many birthdays you've had; believe me, if I can be successful, it's possible for you too, and it's never too late or too early to begin. As a matter of fact, you are right on time.

It was age twenty-six when I got it! It was the most enlightening time in my life. I was ready for the lesson, and the teacher came. I understood why the way I'd been doing it hadn't worked; why many well-meaning people often go wrong; why I was always one day behind my prosperity; and what to do to make permanent positive changes. After many hard knocks, I finally got the life I desired.

You now hold in your hands my special notes in their entirety that led me to a successful retirement. I am confident that this book will impact your life positively from this day forward. Within these pages, it is with great joy that I share with you every tool and insight that empowered me to lead a life I love. Here you will learn how to avoid the common mistakes that keep people stuck in a rut and locked out of abundance. All of the principles here worked for me, but please feel free to take, embrace and adopt from them what serves you best. The goal is to customize and shape your life until it is something you are delighted with!

This book is your exclusive copy. Own it. Put your name in it and prepare to mark, highlight, underline or note the parts that speak to you and your unique circumstances. I'm excited for you because I know this process works. You just have to be willing to work the process. Dust off your dreams, have a little bit of faith, fasten your seat belts and prepare for take off... it's your turn!

I will be right here with you every step of the way, but please be mindful that I can't do it for you. I'm up for the challenge of coaching you through, and I'm confident that I can; but I need you to show up with your firm commitment in order for us to really get you where you want to be.

I will be honest with you, being successful is not easy, but it is simple. Know that each victory along the way will be moving you closer and closer to your champion life. But now promise me that if at any point along this journey you become discouraged, you will remember that any mission worth its pursuit is toughest in the beginning. Should such a time arrive, I encourage you to hold on. Stay focused and pace yourself, but whatever you do, keep moving. It will be worth it. Do yourself a favor and give your dreams another chance. You deserve it. And thank you so much for allowing me to be a part of your success. Now let's get busy once and for all!

Maximum Respect,

Ashu

How I Retired at 26!™

A step-by-step guide
to assessing your freedom
and wealth at any age.

Asha Tyson

ATD Publishing

CHAPTER 1

When Born to Win,
But Left to Lose
(Part 1)

My greatest challenge right now is just trying to wrap my brain around this big blessing of a new life. Just when I think this has to be as good as it gets, I'm wrong, and life gets even better. Rumor had it, I'd done the "Jeffersons' thing," and "moved on up to the east side to a deluxe apartment in the sky."

They were saying I had done well for myself...even got my own dot com. And they always knew I could do it. Funny thing is, no one ever let on.

Really now, who could have known when I was a child, alone in a homeless shelter, that one day the phones would ring off the hook, that there would be a demand for my time, and that media interviews, book signings and extraordinary opportunities from all over the country would overwhelm the calendar and mount up on my desk?

I gotta tell you; I still think about how it came to this: *Me*, this life—complete with a solid state of well being. You know, good health, loving relationships, self-expression and financial freedom...*retirement*. None of it is less than a miracle when you consider where I started.

There was very little evidence in my youth that supported a life of promise. But my story, like that of many other successful people, will demonstrate that it doesn't matter where you begin. Your past, your misfortunes, your circumstances don't define you—unless *you* let them.

Being the only child to a dying single mother was my introduction to the meaning and reality of *challenge*. Momma often reminded me how lucky I was she kept me in the first place. When I was born, the people at the hospital told her that she couldn't handle a child, being sick and all, but Momma was determined. Besides, the very last thing she would do was give away *his* baby.

D-daddy, as I called him, was a ruggedly handsome man, with a solid build, bowed legs and masculine hands that Momma insisted on keeping manicured. His congenial face, peppered with freckles, housed his dimples and sported a bushy mustache. Thirteen years her senior, D-daddy could look like a distinguished gentlemen—that is, when he felt like it.

You see, he had "make or break" features. He could precision cut his full head of hair, shave close, suit up, splash down in smell goods and look like an accomplished man. Or he could let himself go and look like a classic bum in a liquor store, begging for soda pop cans. This exceptionally bright man—philosophical, articulate and charismatic—was a mild-mannered, smooth-talking crooner who could convince an insecure woman of anything. Confident women, however, said he was "full of sh-t."

Everyone, men and women alike, had strong opinions about D-daddy. Mostly, the talk was, "He's really smart, and he'd be okay if he would quit chasing skirts, stop talking about what he's going to do and just do it."

The talk was true.

D-daddy had big plans, huge dreams and grand ideas. Unfortunately, he also had irregular employment, no describable business and no profession to speak of. And yes, D-daddy was a very loving man. He was loving and fertilizing women all throughout the metropolitan area.

Ironically, I have solid memories of feeling loved the first few years of my life. Whenever D-daddy stopped through to visit us, it was always memorable. I can remember...the birthday party they arranged and had featured in the local newspaper for no other reason than I was born; I remember D-daddy falling asleep on Christmas morning while fully disguised as Santa Claus; Momma's tuna sandwiches we snacked on between amusement rides at the state fair; D-daddy preaching at storefront churches; and enjoying rice-n-milk with him after initially being reluctant to try the stuff for fear that it would taste nasty. I remember the stops at McDonald's and being told, as we rode passed Wayne State University, that I was smart enough to go to college and become a lawyer. I remember him entertaining Momma and me with his yodeling and impromptu song writing.

D-daddy could really sing; he had sung professionally, back in his heyday, but never managed to get his big break in the music industry. Anyway, he was a hit with me and Momma. She even made him promise to sing her favorite song at her funeral. Although I hadn't fully come to terms with what "Momma's funeral" meant, I heard her remind him to sing her special song so many times, that I started reminding him too.

Momma, who was the oldest of a bunch of kids, frequently exchanged words with members of her family about their derogatory comments:

"You think that child is better than everybody else, but you'll see. She ain't gone be no better than that no-good-for-nothin' daddy of hers!" Because of their disapproval of him and her personal mission to raise her child without their help, she gave them limited access to me.

"Don't touch my baby; just look!" she would tell them. She had even embarrassed them a few times in front of their friends. "I don't know where their lips have been, so I don't want them kissing on my child!"

Momma usually said exactly what she meant. Sometimes she was tactful; most times she wasn't. Although she was considered generous, "free-hearted" as some called it, heads would roll immediately if you rubbed her the wrong way.

You know how it is, sometimes, after someone has said something that doesn't sit well with you, and later you wish you had taken up for yourself or defended yourself better? We don't think of how to respond, until after it's over, right? Sometimes we try to recreate the situation and say what we feel the next time we see the insulter, but it usually doesn't work as well as we had planned. Well, Momma never had that problem.

She was one of those people who could find the right throat-cutting words, guaranteed to reduce your pride, in the exact moment you offended her. And if the words didn't cut your throat, she had no problem using a kitchen knife! She did, however, have more patience with men.

Around them, her demeanor was docile and submissive, especially with D-daddy; that is, unless he really made her mad. In that case, he too could find himself in the emergency room with a stab wound or some kind of closed head injury.

This temper was housed in a small and feminine frame with long, thin limbs. Momma didn't look at all like a terminally ill person. She appeared healthy and normal. She was dainty and shapely with large eyes and a smile that started out higher on one side than the other. Some people thought she favored Diana Ross, but everyone, even strangers on the street, acknowledged her perfect skin.

Momma's flawless face was like caramel-colored porcelain on which she never wore any make-up. Her beauty regimen consisted of very little. After applying a sheer coat of chapstick to her lips, she used her slender fingers to swoop and poise her black mane into its trademark bun. Finally, she polished off her "do" with pressing oil. Then, she was ready to leave the house. Speaking of the house...

We lived in the upstairs portion of a three-bedroom, two-family flat in Detroit's inner city. Although it wasn't the best, and the landlady didn't seem to care about us sharing the place with rats and roaches, Momma didn't complain. She took pride in keeping the place neat and clean. Every hardwood floor was buffed to a high gloss. She even made the curtains and throw pillows herself. We had nothing but old furniture, all secondhand stuff D-daddy found, but she made the best of it.

D-daddy was always finding things on the streets. He was a proud treasure hunter. On any given day, you could see him on top of a pile of garbage that someone had left to be dumped. People called him a "junkman," but he didn't seem to concern himself with what others thought—especially when it came to raising me.

D-daddy had a controversial parenting style that old fashioned disciplinarians despised. They thought I needed more chastising than what he was giving. While D-daddy was encouraging me to be a thinker, expressive and free, other adults were saying,"Children ought to be seen, not heard."

I stayed in trouble over that one.

I talked constantly, nonstop, always and forever. I talked about anything and everything without fail. I asked questions, gave answers and took great delight in being inquisitive. Because of this, I was always being told to take my little tail somewhere and sit down, shut up and stay out of the way. This was very difficult for me, given my energy level, so before long, I was labeled "bad." D-daddy would tell people not to call me that, but when he wasn't around, they did it as though someone had paid them.

The other adults didn't like that D-daddy allowed me to say the words *lie* and *liar* either. They said, for a child, it was like cursing. And I should say "story" instead. D-daddy thought calling deception a "story" was foolish for anyone of any age.

"Stories are in story books and that's fair game—honest fiction," D-daddy would lecture, "...but a lie is a lie, and if you are not telling the truth, you are indeed lying."

D-daddy supported his teachings by using the Bible. I could say anything written in there as long as it was used in its proper context. D-daddy said,"the Bible says, 'All liars shall have their part in the lake.'" D-daddy would continue with passion, "It didn't say anything about all *story* tellers!"

Meanwhile, Momma didn't care what D-daddy taught me, even when it went against the grain of her own strict upbringing. As long as he kept coming around, she was smiling. Unfortunately, she would soon stop.

D-daddy, with his typical MIA (Missing In Action) demeanor, had always been preoccupied. He never slept in a bed or wore pajamas. Instead he snoozed, fully dressed in our dark brown pleather chair that had tape on the arm. He was always ready to go.

Where, you ask?

Who knew?

It was as though he lived with his jacket on and keys in his hand. That was just D-daddy's way, and I was used to it. But something began to change.

D-daddy visited less and never stayed long. His drop-ins

became more infrequent and finally ceased altogether—no calls, letters, nothing. D-daddy was gone.

––––––––––––––––––––

Momma's hospital visits grew closer together now and lasted anywhere from two weeks to a month. In the hospital, out of the hospital, in three weeks, out three weeks. Back in, back out. This was our life.

Although most of her attacks happened at home, she could suddenly be stricken with pain anytime, anyplace. Her cries were like thunder that came from the bottom of her soul. She would fall to her knees, lie on her face and grovel to God. She would lose all composure and toss wildly, rocking herself back and forth on the shiny floors. Her body was doubled over in a knot while she wailed and cried out for help. Momma, with her piercing screams, begged for mercy as though someone had set her on fire, but she couldn't run and she couldn't die. Her smooth face was wet with sweat. And tears poured from her yellow eyes. I couldn't do anything to help Momma. No one could. The only thing to do was execute The Plan.

I knew it well. I had been trained how to kick into emergency mode by age four. My moves were experienced and well versed. I was careful not to miss a step, mindful to remain calm and attentive to the fact that Momma's life was at stake. While she endured agony, I used a chair to reach the butterscotch colored phone mounted on the kitchen wall.

Press 911. Tell them that she is having a "crisis." I'd been taught to give the address, complete with landmarks. There were only five houses on each side of our block, and we were hard to find. Our place was isolated, tucked away. Unless you knew exactly where you were going, you would never get there. Nothing drove down our street, for the most part, not even the ice cream truck. Many of the paramedics who had been successful said that they found us because I had told them we were wedged between two alleys. I was always so proud of being helpful.

After hanging up with the dispatcher, my next step was to call the relatives who hadn't been allowed to love me. I never wanted to, but I had no choice. I didn't know their phone number by heart, but I knew the pattern. It was round with a dip at the top.

Next, it was time to help Momma put clothes on her aching body. I was gentle. Even while distressed and in pain, Momma always thanked me for getting her dressed. I then pushed her heavy suitcase, which was always packed with a surplus of sleepwear, to the front door. Then I sat still—quiet, numb, waiting. The house was silent as I listened only to the sounds of suffering coming from my tortured momma.

Grandma said that I needed to be taken down a "button hole lower." "Your Momma and your ol' daddy thought too much of you, but now you wit me. Let's see how you do when it ain't so rosy." At Grandma's, I got the old-fashioned, body, mind, spirit-breaking child-rearing—the way it "should have been done in the first place," according to her.

"That say-what-you-feel-mess your Momma and daddy let you do, ain't gonna happen here!" And it was so. Grandma didn't believe in children having a mind or asking questions. Even your feelings weren't your own. You were allowed only three emotions: guilt, shame and fear. Anger, disappointment, sadness, joy, and even pain were forbidden.

This was it for me. Punishment. For what, I didn't know.

What I knew was that Daddy, who I no longer called D-daddy, had abandoned us completely. And aside·from the

24

connection Momma and I had during the pre-hospital ritual, she had become distant. So, each and every time Momma got sick, I was left alone to feel the wrath of the only family I had. So, there I was. Vulnerable. Instead of being nurtured, I was going to learn what it meant to feel blackballed.

Grandma kept her promise and was successful. She'd fully achieved her goal of making me feel worthless and like an outsider in their home. I wasn't allowed any of my own clothing. Instead, I was told to wear my aunt's clothes. This wouldn't have been a problem except I was a skinny child, while my aunt, being three years older, was much "healthier" and taller. Her clothes hung off of me like I hadn't put anything at all inside of them. Grandma kept the clothes from falling off by radically securing them with extra large safety pins or strings. Talk about feeling like a *misfit*.

Maybe the clothes wouldn't have felt so awkward had I been allowed to bathe first, but there was no shower, and the tub wasn't used for anything other than storage. It always had stuff in it—clothes, mops, buckets, washboards, just stuff. So, I "washed-up" at the face bowl as instructed, but I felt dirty. In my mind, they thought that I was too insignificant to take a bath.

Having to use my underwear to "wash-up" didn't help any, but it was better than sharing wash cloths with all the others. Grandma's duplex wasn't much bigger than our flat, and it was always very crowded. So resources, linen and most other stuff were always in short supply.

Grandma was a round, stout woman with chestnut brown eyes and a wholesome face. I found it most fascinating that her belly would jiggle like jello when she laughed heartily. The ashes from her cigarette would land right on that stomach every time. I would watch to see them fall. That was the extent of the entertainment there, and that was over when she stopped smoking.

Food was scarce, but Grandma was very talented at "making do." She would supplement meals with sugar sandwiches, or sometimes my cousins and I would split a vienna sausage down the long way and roll it into a single slice of white bread. Because the only thing available to the children was water, Grandma would creatively make sugar-water or evaporated milk-water. And there we were, children full of sweeteners, sitting absolutely still on the front porch and knowing that moving, without being called upon, would be detrimental.

Grandma made homemade biscuits from scratch every Saturday morning. Biscuits were the highlight of the day because there would be no cartoon watching, outings, or games. Grandma's house was not for children; looking around the place, you wouldn't think they even knew any kids. The house belonged to Granddad and him alone.

No one ate these hot buttered biscuits with Granddad's syrup; anything of Grandma's was free to everyone, but everything of his was off limits. No one got in his way or said anything other than, "Yes, sir."

I wasn't sure why, but Granddad was a very special man—above all others.

He had a common face that was the shade of coffee with no cream or sugar. You could find his not-so-unique features many times over throughout the black community. He looked like a lot of other middle-aged colored men who wore glasses and were from the South, came north after the war, and found work in a factory. Although not attractive, he was a sharp dresser, and he knew it. For some reason, we had been trained to worship him, but we all called it respect. Granddad was second to no one on earth or in heaven. And he knew that too.

When you entered the house, you were expected to bow. As you did, he tilted his dark cheek to receive a kiss. If he walked in the house and you were in his chair, you had to rise and surrender it before he approached. No one was allowed to eat until Granddad had been served, typically on his green and blue flowered tin tray. He never asked for anything nor did he thank anyone; he ordered you and you got it. Granddad was not a man of words. He grunted, flagged or gestured without eye contact, and you were supposed to know what it all meant. He only smiled when posing for family pictures, and he only laughed when someone made fun of Grandma. Then he would throw his head back, showing his gold tooth, and let out a steady ha-ha with such force that it caused his whole body to shift from one side to the other.

Granddad wasn't affectionate, especially with children. There were, however, some kids he was willing to tolerate more than others. If he was sort of fond of you, he'd slip you change for the ice cream truck, which did drive down Grandma's street. I never got anything from his heavy pocket full of jingle. And neither he nor Grandma were shy about telling you that you weren't the favorite child. They didn't feel pressured to keep things fair between the kids either. When the other children were off doing fun things like maybe visiting Edge Water Park, they were always short one ticket. Sometimes they'd go to Tracy's Party Store for candy or downtown to shop on Woodward Avenue. I never knew why, but I just couldn't go.

Instead, I stayed at the house with Grandma and Granddad. The house felt empty. With nothing else to do, I'd gently climb up on the light blue plastic covered sofa, so not to disturb Granddad's evening news with the crunch of my movement. During commercials, I'd try to talk with him, but he would grumble something about me talking too much and motion me away. I guess I was rambling on rather quickly, trying to get it all in before the news came back on. As usual, after being scolded for my big mouth, I'd go somewhere out of the way, sit down and hush. While being as still as I could, I heard only two sounds: Grandma whirling around the kitchen preparing to feed Granddad, and him rubbing his silver, flaky bare feet together while anticipating the forthcoming meal that would truly be fit for a king. Maybe if I behaved, Grandma would have me do something really important like carry his ice tea or hot sauce bottle. If not, I would just avoid being a bother.

No one watched Granddad's floor model television except him — unless he was gone. Then five or six of us would beg Grandma to let us turn on the set and steal a few moments of a good movie. We all knew that the minute he walked in the door, even before taking off his coat, he would bend his tall, lean body down to flick the channel to the news or the "ball game." While some of us were disappointed almost to tears, we dared not say a word! Instead, we'd defenselessly drag ourselves out of the room, one by one, pack tightly into our designated sleeping spaces and hope to hear how the movie ended in school the next day. Sometimes, I would create the ending I thought the movie should have as I fell asleep.

One of the many times, while he was reaching to change the station in front of us, I found the courage to look into his stern face. I wondered if he was capable of having enough compassion to change his mind if he knew how glad it would make my heart to sit there swallowed in those big clothes and see just one movie. He actually looked a bit hesitant to flip the switch, but he did it anyway.

Maybe Granddad had been trained to be ornery as much as we had been trained to fear and obey. Being mean was his comfort zone now, and contemplating tenderness may have confused him. He may not have known how to feel anything other than meanness.

I don't know whether Grandma knew it or not, but she was the one who decided what everybody felt in that house—including him. Sure enough, Granddad was the boss, but Grandma had the power.

I got fussed out on a daily basis for "igging" him, as he called it (short for ignored). They said I didn't give him his due respect. This was major grounds for being put out of this family. Physical harm would be too good for you should you fail to hail to the chief! And I'd already been on thin ice from the beginning. What no one could see was that I wasn't intentionally being flippant or sassy. I was capable of glorifying Granddad along with the best of 'em, and I was willing. I just didn't understand why we were all doing it. I wanted badly to get in on the act like everyone else; it may have even meant I would deserve ice cream money some day. But I just didn't know what the act was about. I'm not sure if anyone else knew either, but they had been smart enough not to question it. They would just obey.

Then one day, it occurred to me! Maybe Granddad had done something miraculous before I was born that I didn't know about. Maybe he had been a war hero and saved the lives of an entire platoon or something. Perhaps he had been a prophet down south and was able to circumvent catastrophe with his visions of what was to come. Maybe my Granddaddy helped pioneer the Civil Rights Movement and now, because of his efforts, I wouldn't see a "colored only" sign a day in my life!

I decided to risk being crucified and ask Grandma why Granddad was Lord. Surprisingly, she answered, as though it should have been obvious.

29

"He's a good provider!" She exclaimed. "Daddy," as she called him, "never raised a hand to me, and he takes care of this family."

I waited patiently, just in case Grandma had forgotten something. After a few minutes of quietness, I realized she was done.

So that was it. He provided. Granddad had provided shelter like a worker bee.

I was never really able to step into the fullness of the worship thing after that. It didn't feel normal. I thought we were spreading the royal treatment on a little thick for someone who was paying bills and not beating up Grandma. I did think Granddad was pretty smart though. You would have to be a genius to pass off below average performance as superior. What's more, he had brainwashed his entire family into buying it! I was truly impressed. He didn't have to be considerate, cordial or even mindful that anyone else lived in the house, and still he was receiving the honors of a blue-blooded legend. Without uttering as much as a sentence, he had a full staff of servants prepared to jump, sacrifice and comply with his every command. How Granddad did it, I didn't know, but it was brilliant.

Grandma and the relatives would compare them—my daddy and the Provider. They would laugh and talk about how irresponsible Daddy was.

"All he 's ever done was make babies."

I would reply as wisely as I could, "Granddad made a bunch too."

They would respond with victory, "The difference is he takes care of his!"

I had been defeated; it was all true. Daddy had a slew of kids, although the last census estimated the number to be around 19, Daddy claims 14. The actual count remains unknown. Few, if any, of the children received support from him, financial or otherwise. A group of us were part of his special namesake tribe. That meant your name began with "Er" like his. Mine was Ernetta. There was a second Ernetta for whatever reason, who was also his daughter, but she had a different mother. Most of us had different mothers. There were some other "Ers,"somewhere — some dead, some alive. While Daddy gave a great deal of attention to giving first names, none of us, whether we were "Er" or not, had his last name. On second thought, he gave the last few kids his last name after their mother died so that the Social Security Office wouldn't be suspicious about why he was cashing the checks. No matter who the mother was, all of us were born out of wedlock. And so, we were bastards according to the Provider.

They continuously challenged me about Daddy. They went on and on about how he stood around, always in people's faces, trying to sound deep and couldn't keep a decent running car...how he was a womanizer, a liar, a cheat, and "worse than an infidel." I couldn't uphold him by myself, and I couldn't keep up. Everyone talked at once, except when they took turns taking individual cracks at him. The things they said made sense. I wanted to love Daddy and stand up for him, but I didn't even know where he was. Defending him was hard and getting harder. These were adults and they were witty; I, on the other hand, was in the third grade, and I just didn't know what to say to them. When they talked about my gullible mother and my "rollin' stone papa," the truth was in my face. They were right. I wasn't part of anything or anybody special. Daddy had voluntarily vanished. Momma was forced to make breathing her first priority, and no one at Grandma's house liked me.

There was one accommodation made for me at Grandma's—Momma's hospital phone number. Someone always wrote it really large and put it by the telephone so that I could freely call her.

When I called Momma, she told me a little about her roommates, the hospital food and gifts she bought for me off the toy cart. When the doctor came in, she'd have to hang up. When I didn't have her to talk to anymore, I'd disappear off into a corner somewhere and try not to become talkative and worrisome.

Sometimes, I would get to visit Momma. I spent years sneaking up to her room and feeling like a hardened criminal for it. The hospital had age restrictions, and I was always too young to visit my mother on her sick bed, which is where she lived more often than she lived with me.

Once, I asked Momma what this sickness was that had so much control over us. Sickle cell anemia, she explained, was inherited from Grandma and the Provider. Instead of her cells being soft, like jelly in a sandwich bag and round like Grandma's phone number, her cells were shaped like bananas and hard like legos. When her cells got caught and tangled in her joints, it hurt beyond imagining. Momma said her blood was no good, and when she went to the hospital all the time, it was to get some more. I asked Momma if she was going to die.

"Yeah!" she announced, as though it were a stupid question.

I was devastated! Daddy was gone, and now I wouldn't have her either.

"When?" I wanted her to tell me not to worry and that she would be with me a long time.

Instead, she said, "I don't know. It could happen at anytime, probably when you least expect it."

I became overwhelmed with silent terror from that day forward. What if she died in her sleep or while I was in school or while she was in the hospital? I didn't see any time as a good one for this to happen! In an instant, Momma had given me a lifetime of enormous burden. At night, I checked her constantly to see if she was breathing. I lived preoccupied with the agonizing anticipation of her death, and her funeral. During the day, ringing telephones made me jump because at anytime I knew it could be The Call. Then at night there were the reoccurring nightmares. Secret anxiety had become my life because, by this time, I understood death.

A schoolmate of mine had been killed in a house fire, and the class was taken to the funeral. I didn't touch the dead body, but another girl did. She said he was cold; I believed her. He looked cold, stiff, lifeless, and nothing at all like when we were all on the playground. Now I knew when I found Momma, she would be cold.

I began checking every morning to to see if Momma was cold. I decided that when I found her, I would cover her with a blanket. Then I'd go somewhere, sit down and be quiet. They wouldn't have to worry about me talking. I wouldn't say a word, and I wouldn't move. I wouldn't call anyone because I knew they would come for me, and I didn't want to go. It wouldn't be so bad if it were Daddy, but it wouldn't be him. It was never him.

I worried endlessly. I feared not having enough money to pay for her funeral. I feared not being able to find Daddy to sing her favorite song. Maybe I would have to sing it, but I wasn't sure if I remembered the words. I feared living at Grandma's. There was so much on my mind. I was haunted by the fear of finding Momma cold. As the years passed, I stressed all of my days and nights about finding her cold. And eventually, I did.

CHAPTER 2

When Born to Win, But Left to Lose
(Part 2)

Momma wasn't dead, but she was cold. She was cold and angry all the time. I felt like someone who Momma didn't like anymore. She would tell anybody who would listen—strangers at the bus stop, at the doctor's office or anywhere else she struck up a conversation—how much trouble I was. She seemed to be annoyed by the thought of me. I had become stupid and ugly to her, and she had developed a daily mantra of calling me names, wishing me dead and cursing my life.

"People are always talking about child abuse, child abuse, child abuse! What about parent abuse?" Momma yelled. "Your ass always needin' things—shoes, clothes, attention...I'm sick of you!"

People rarely came around us; according to Momma, that was my fault. Every once in a while, one of the aunts would come and take my cousin and me out for dinner, to a movie or to the arcade. I lived for those interludes, but for the most part, Momma and I were alone. And even though I was afraid of her and she was disgusted at the sight of me, we were all we had.

"I ought to throw you over a bridge or just leave here and never come back like your daddy did!" Momma would say. She told me that I had run my father away.

"You are the reason I can't get or keep a man. I have had nothing but bad luck since you got here!"

A woman Momma met in the hospital had sickle cell and one daughter, just like Momma. Unlike Momma, this woman had recently married a doctor. I didn't know why Momma hadn't done that. Surely she had seen plenty of them during all of her hospital visits.

I honestly couldn't remember running any of Momma's male friends away. I thought that the Baptist church deacon left because he decided to go ahead and marry the lady he had been living with all along. The gang leader had to go into hiding because someone was trying to kill him; and the forty-year-old who lived with his mother stopped coming around after getting Momma pregnant. He may have never left had he known the baby would die like most of Momma's babies did.

I was actually her sixth child out of about eight. But being an only survivor was no picnic; it came with the great burden of always hearing Momma tell me that the wrong child lived.

Every day was a battle. Aside from Momma's fussing, hissing and cursing, there was also the battering. Being hit without warning was such a large part of my life that I grew immune to it. I had no idea what peace felt like.

Sometimes I ran from her while she was trying to punch, slap or kick me, and she would unsuccessfully chase me. When she gave up, I thought it was over. But later that night after I'd fallen asleep Momma would tie me to the bed with jute rope. Then she would strike me unmercifully with braided branches from a small tree until she was tired or until I passed out.

It wasn't unusual for me to be thrashed through windows or doors. I dodged many chairs, ashtrays and flatware.

Sometimes I was lucky because she missed. Other times I wasn't.

Terms or acts of endearment didn't happen with Momma. I didn't lay on her lap, and we didn't hug. Whenever I said I loved her, she accused me of lying and started in on me again with the clobbering. So I stopped saying it.

Momma was always upset, and nothing I did or didn't do helped. When I lied, I got beatings. When I told the truth, I got beatings. I never knew what to do to please her or what I had done to displease her.

Between being drenched in the backwash of Momma's rage and going back and forth to Grandma's, I was constantly bed-wetting, losing my eyeglasses, getting poor grades, fighting with other kids, getting expelled, and being called a "disruptive, insubordinate problem child."

I was sent to the principal's office more often than he actually came to work. He took vacation and sick days; I didn't. They called me a busybody. I was getting out of my seat without permission, disturbing the other children while they were trying to do their class work, and, of course, talking too much—always talking too much. By this time, they had even nicknamed me "motor mouth" which was later upgraded to "mouth mobile."

I was sent to counselors and tested for attention disorders. They always determined the results the same; I was just "bad," and nothing or no one could "fix" me. I'd convinced myself that both Momma and I would be better off if I ran away, so I did.

One Christmas Eve, I didn't want to risk being caught leaving, so I didn't grab a coat. I put a grape sucker underneath my green and red tightly woven knit hat and ran down the cold city streets.

I had no clue where I was headed. I ended up lost and

scared. A woman and her child found me sitting on the ground crying. The seat of my clothes were wet from snow, and my fingers didn't feel like part of my body anymore. I ached for both warmth and a safe, new home.

The woman took me into a local bar. There weren't many people in there. I guess with it being Christmas Eve, folks weren't drinking as much as they were shopping.

After the lady called the police, she left. The bartender gave me orange juice and billiard lessons as we waited. Eventually the cops came and took me back to Momma.

There, Grandma and a few of the aunts had already prepared themselves to take my head off. Grandma volunteered to hand out my punishment—as a favor to Momma. I had no idea what my fate would be, but one thing was for sure: if Grandma was handling it, I was doomed!

The ride to Grandma's was cluttered with comments about my demonic behavior.

Once we arrived at the red and white house that Granddad was so proud of, I sat quietly. The house was fairly noisy from the incoming and outgoing traffic. After what seemed to be an eternity, everything became still. Everyone had left except Grandma and me.

"Come on," Grandma demanded while leading the way to the back of the house. I could feel a lump in my throat and somewhere in the recesses of my mind, I could hear the words "dead child walking."

Once we reached the end of the green mile, Grandma took a large jar of Vaseline from the cabinet. She popped the lid off and looked at me. My eyes grew large from anxiety. What was she doing? Grandma then scooped out half of the petroleum jelly and began smearing it all over my face. It was thick enough to slice.

I said, "What are you doing that for, Grandma?" With no reply, she proceeded to escort me to her bedroom, where she took her old washed out, unraveling bra from a drawer.

Grandma then tied a bra that had been designed for her obese body, back and forth around my entire head, making certain to cover my mouth before finally hooking it closed.

The house traffic started up again. Grandma announced that I couldn't speak to anyone except her. I had been forbidden to talk. I had been suspended from life and condemned to remaining greasy while wearing underwear on my face.

The kids laughed. After much pondering, I figured out what Grandma had done. Her intentions were to make me feel unattractive and humiliated with her homemade mummy mask.

What Grandma didn't know was that the whole shame plan wasn't necessary. In her home, I had felt as valuable as the bra, with its hanging strings, for all eight of my years. I thought if God really loved me He would have let me stay at the bar for Christmas—no Grandma's house, no Momma's house, no school.

School was another matter. There, I was positioned away from the classroom unit. That meant that my permanent seat was in a corner or behind a screen somewhere away from the other children. Oddly enough, that sometimes worked out for the best because I wouldn't have to hear the kids teasing me about my clothes. They ragged on me badly and constantly. It had been a daily ritual.

We just didn't have the money for clothes. Momma was totally disabled and hadn't been able to work since before I was born, but she desperately wanted to and was jealous of anyone who could. Social Security was our sole means of income, and although she kept me very neat and clean with the assistance of a state provided housekeeper, my clothes were terribly outdated and too small.

I decided to tell the other kids the truth about why I dressed the way that I did. I thought they would understand. *Wrong!*

The truth just gave them more material to use against me. Now, in addition to the attacks on my attire, I had to hear about my lazy mother who pretended to be sick in order to get welfare. Their comments came without fail, and I wouldn't get a break from the taunting because I would never wear anything acceptable; I just didn't own it. At home, the clothes I wore were too little, and at Grandma's, they were too big. Either way, for years, I would be a joke.

Designer clothes were something beyond imagining, but I did not pout or whine about not having them. Instead, I ignored the secret longing I had for wearing a pair of pants, at least once, that went past my ankles instead of stopping two inches above them. But I dared not complain. I didn't want to upset Momma and get her started in on me with the nagging and wailing. Besides, I wanted to believe that she would have done better if the resources were there.

A few times I told her about the daily teasing in school. She said to ignore them and to say: "At least I'm clean." Often, Momma girded me with lame comebacks that didn't comfort or empower me at all. When I used them, it made matters worse. Children considered "clean" a given not a bonus. "Sticks and stones can break my bones, but words will never hurt me," also got me eaten alive! I stopped informing Momma. I didn't need snappy replies; I really needed clothes that actually fit my body. She couldn't provide them; so I just dealt with it all silently and daydreamed of living Gina's life.

Gina was a classmate who lived around the corner, but didn't play with me, participate in the class Halloween parties, or accept birthday cards.

Adults said Gina was "good." I figured if I hung around her, I would be good too. I wanted people to be as kind to me as they were to her, so I watched how she behaved in school. She was quiet and reserved, and she colored softly inside of the lines.

We walked home from school together every now and then. On the few occasions I visited her home, I paid close attention to how she and her parents got along.

They talked calmly, asked her things, and let her choose the contents of her lunch. Everybody there seemed happy to see Gina...*What was this?*

I didn't know that people could actually want their kids! At my house, I had only known feelings of being "in the way." I felt like something that Momma wanted at first, changed her mind, but went ahead and followed through with since the damage was already done.

Gina's mom would give me little magazines about God—whom they didn't call God. I got the feeling that I would be good enough to play with Gina if only I could be a good little girl and stop loving Christmas.

One day, while being invited to the Kingdom Hall by Gina's mom and dad, I lost track of time and was late getting home from school!

Momma was going to have my head on a platter, and neither God nor Jehovah could stop the wrath of Momma!

Momma told me to never come home from school late and always walk in a group with other kids. "Walking alone invites potential trouble with strangers," she said.

I was convinced that Momma was just making things up. No one we knew or ever met wanted me, so why would some stranger? Sometimes Momma says the silliest things, I thought to myself.

In my mind, other people thought I was unlovable and unworthy of being kidnapped. If by chance a stranger had snatched me, once he realized it was me (the notorious bad seed) and not Gina (the golden love child) he would return

41

me, complete with a note of apology pinned to my shirt. Or maybe police would find him stretched out somewhere, lifeless and stiff because I had talked him to death.

At any rate, no one teased Gina, not that anyone could. She always wore designer clothes in her own size.

Once Momma and I went to a department store, but this trip was unlike any other. I had seen the designer clothes many times before and as usual, ignored them. There was no use pining. I knew the deal: we couldn't "afford" it. This particular time, I guess the pressure of being ridiculed had come to a head. Never wearing anything that met the standards of my peers had gotten the best of me, and unlike all the other times, I couldn't and didn't want to understand that we couldn't "afford" it.

I was feeling overwhelmed by the years of constant teasing and pent-up anger. I lost my composure, and before I knew it, I was calling out to her.

"Momma."

She turned around.

"What!"

I couldn't say a word. The very next move I made was uncharacteristic and surprising even to me. Before I had time to put my thoughts into some kind of order, I had fallen to my knees. It wasn't a tantrum or an attempt to embarrass her, and I think she knew that. I was on an entirely different frequency from that of a spoiled child throwing a fit. Besides, that kind of behavior just wasn't my style.

I tuned out the world and reached for my mother. I looked into her eyes with a sincerity I had never experienced. There was no shame or pride in my thoughts—only meekness. I had humbled myself to the very essence of my human vulnerability, and gently—so very gently—I begged my mother for a pair of jeans.

Shoppers were now looking on, but I couldn't worry about them. I was communicating with my mother, and I'd never done that before, not with my soul.

In the one single moment that I had her undivided attention, I tried to make her understand all I felt and had been feeling for years. I thought I would burst. My heart overflowed with emotions that I was incapable of articulating. My anguish ran far too deep, and I didn't know the words to express them. All my thoughts were jumbled together and stuck inside my head. My motor mouth had failed me completely, so my tears spoke instead:

Momma please love me and make me feel safe. I'm sorry you're sick. I miss you when you're in the hospital, and I pray all the time for your healing. I'm not the holy terror that everyone thinks I am. I want to be "good" in school and I try, but I don't know what "good" means. I'm tired of being considered the "behavior problem" by my teachers. I have done my best to be strong when you're ill, and it hurts that no one acknowledges my courage. As mean as you have been to me, you are all I have. I love you and you're dying. That burden is heavy, and I have nightmares about it all the time. I want people to see my innocence. I am afraid of the dark, and you say it is because I'm "bad," but I don't think so Momma. I think it's because after one of the aunts hits me with her big, brown, wooden scissors that she uses to pick things up with, she locks me in the closet at Grandma's house.

I have tried to kill myself — not because I don't want to live, but because I don't want to live with a mother who is mad at me for being healthy. My very existence provides the material for classroom mockery daily, hourly. It never stops. Authority figures don't protect me because they consider me to be the little demon who's getting what she deserves. I want to be valued enough to get a break from the teasing. I want to sit with the rest of the class and not off to the side like some contagious freak. I want to stop being afraid of you. I want you to allow the old marks and bruises to heal before you put fresh ones on my body. I want someone to

43

understand why I talk so much, and then calmly and patiently explain it to me. I want somebody in this world to love me enough to spend thirty-six dollars on a pair of jeans in my own size, and Momma, I want that somebody to be you.

I managed to open my mouth and in the faintest whisper say, "I will never ask for anything else from you as long as I live, but I need these jeans, please. Momma, *please.*

Briefly, I could see my mother's humanism even as she snapped the words:

"Girl, hurry up and get those pants and come on." She headed hastily towards the register still snapping, "I'm ready to go!"

My excitement coupled with the fear she might change her mind caused me to grab the wrong pair; it wasn't the pair I had envisioned all those years, but it didn't matter. I got Gloria Vanderbilt jeans that day because my mother sensed my need.

I wore those pants until they fell apart, and I never forgot my promise to her. After that time, she gave me special occasion gifts and granted three separate loans throughout the years, but never again did I ask her for anything.

I didn't have to ask for church clothes. Momma saw to it that I was adequately dressed for church. I liked church; the kids there didn't tease me, and I felt useful. I sang in the children's choir and somehow, without any effort, became the designated "speaker" for every event.

It all started with someone giving me a poem to learn like all the other kids at Easter time. Then I was given longer poems than everyone else. After some time, I was told to memorize entire passages out of the Bible.

By age nine, I was narrating plays and giving keynote addresses at banquet halls for award and appreciation ceremonies. Some of those events didn't even permit children, but because I was the speaker, I was in the house!

It made Momma so proud of me.

Many times she would arrange a temporary release to leave the hospital and see me perform. She would always have to go back immediately after the event, but I was thrilled to see her there. Sometimes the doctor didn't approve her pass; she was just too ill.

"Find an empty seat, and pretend I'm there with you," Momma said.

Occasionally, when she said she couldn't make it, I would scan the audience to find the chair that would represent her.

At that moment I would receive an incredible surprise!

It was the woman who frightened me more than anything else in the world. It was Momma! But she wasn't making me afraid. Instead she was sitting in the front pew smiling at me! There she was with her small hand aggressively waving my way. I beamed. It was really Momma! She had pleaded and bargained with the doctor in order to get her pass approved. She wouldn't be able to stay until the end of the program; she would have to go back into the hospital the second I finished giving my presentation, but I was happy she came at all. I then made it my business to earn a standing ovation so that when Momma made her exit she would not be a spectacle.

Every now and then, I would see Daddy, but never at any of my performances. We'd bump into him and his newest family at the grocery store, or someone would see him just *out* somewhere. He never had a phone number, and his address changed so frequently that we couldn't keep in contact with him.

Once every three or four months, he would call and make plans to see me. I would sit patiently with my nose pressed against the window, occasionally turning my head from left to right waiting for my daddy. He never came or called.

Momma wasn't cruel to me after Daddy's "no shows." She would say, "Your daddy doesn't mean to disappoint you." Momma never said anything negative about him, and she would defend him every time. Although I was disappointed by all of Daddy's empty promises, whenever I did see him, even months later, I welcomed him just the same.

When I was eleven, Momma met another reverend at a church which aired miracles on TV. We had gone to see if Momma could get healed. He took us home after the broadcast. Soon after, he and Momma became an item.

There was something about him that I wasn't quite comfortable with, but I knew better than to say anything. Momma would have accused me of being jealous of the time she was spending with someone other than me. I really wasn't jealous. I was relieved that she had found a new interest. It put space between the beatings.

Momma and the Reverend sensed that I didn't find him to be the knight in shining armor that she did, so they always spoke of getting married like it was some kind of retaliation against me for disliking him.

She reminded me that it was her life and that it didn't matter what I thought of him. "Now it's my turn to be happy," Momma would say as if everybody else, including me, had already had their turns.

Usually, while the Reverend and Momma were in his bedroom squeaking the springs, I waited downstairs, pacing back and forth, anxious to go home.

His house wasn't much to look at. It was cold and empty, and everything smelled like wood and moth balls. The only decor was Tessie Hill, Shirley Caesar and the people who sang "I'm Climbing Up on the Rough Side of the Mountain." Their album covers were taped to a wall next to hanging stereo speakers in the dining room.

There was no television except for the one upstairs in his bedroom where they were, and I was afraid to knock and ask for it! So instead, I would leave the house. When I returned hours later, it didn't matter. They never noticed I had left.

I didn't go far; I'd take walks to the neighborhood park and lie to children about who my parents were. My folks were always some successful couple who lived in the suburbs, and I was an only child who went to private school. I was a hit at the swings. The children there were so impressed. Then the time came for them to go home with their parents. Although I knew no one was looking for me, coming for me or even missing me, I decided it was probably best that I headed back too; it was getting dark.

After some time, the Reverend moved us away from the only home I'd known, and we stopped going to church. Also, staying at Grandma's during Momma's hospital visits was no longer an option. A twenty-minute drive one way was considered long distance traveling to Granddad, and that was too much just to take me to school.

God knows I didn't want to stay with the Reverend, but having no choice, I tried to convince myself it would be okay. I did have my own room there. Besides that, he had been nice to Momma and me. He started my bottle cap collection; he always took me to the movies, followed by Burger King, and for the first time in my life, I was getting an allowance! Meanwhile, Momma was enjoying the used car and kitchen table he had given her.

Maybe I had been too hard on him. A year had gone by already, and still he was being a pretty nice guy. Aside from my intuition, I had no real reason for not trusting him.

I decided to stop protesting their marriage and enjoy the fact that I was going to get a new father who had a home and a phone number.

Then it happened.

Momma was in the hospital and I was at the Reverend's house asleep in my bed when he came in and climbed on top of me. *What was he doing!* He was moving fast and desperately trying to get under the covers. I held onto them, but he was determined. It was as though he was overtaken by some invisible force that had geared him up to suddenly attack.

Why was he doing this to me! I was confused and uncomfortable. Had something happened in the night? Had he gotten sick, lost his mind and couldn't remember who I was?

I squirmed to get from under him, but I couldn't move. He had stapled me down with his heavy body.

He was breathing hard and his breath smelled bad like mildew and peppermint. He pressed his mouth against mine and tried to push his tongue in. I folded my lips inward and wrapped them around my teeth so hard that it hurt.

He chased the direction of my head as I continued to jerk it from right to left dodging his.

Eventually, he stopped trying to force himself in my mouth in order to move down. I tried to lock, bend and pull my knees into my body, but he was lying on them.

I never said "no," and I didn't say "stop." I didn't know I could. I had been forbidden to say "no" to adults. I hadn't been taught that my feelings, thoughts and body belonged to me, so whether adults were violating me or not, I was not entitled to defend myself.

The only words I could say were, "Why are you doing this to me?" I wanted him to just do the right thing and go away, but I didn't know how to make that happen.

He fumbled to lift my gown and with one hand he snatched my panties down and put *his thing*—as all us kids called it in school—between my thighs. I clinched my legs together and tried to scoot away. Then suddenly, he just can believe what they see, but a wealth building mentality requires believing what is not seen; this is faith. Having faith means knowing, you'll see it when you believe it! The trouble is most people have stopped believing. The pressures of struggling and getting by have worn us out and made us shortsighted. Some have accepted mediocrity as normal, and it shows up even in their conversation. They tend to say things like, "I'm not negative, I'm just being realistic." It's this attitude that breeds limitation. Being "realistic" stifles your imagination.

To live extraordinary, you must allow your creative mind to overpower your logical one. Logic puts strain on dreams and justifies lack. This is how people find themselves stuck. You recognize these people even by the way they physically move. They walk and talk with low energy.

I used to know someone who would call and leave draining messages on my voice mail. Nothing was ever particularly wrong with her; this was just how she responded to life—dry and sluggish. But we must seek to be refreshed with the newness of each and every day.

Give Up the Need to Always Be Right

Let go of what you think stops you. Let go of your doubts, set backs, shortcomings, who you think doesn't like you, what you think isn't fair, your regrets, and your misfortunes. You must be willing to be wrong to allow space for new information. Being "right" about your helplessness is too costly.

Give up useless thought forms. Surrender the current interpretations of what you think has a stranglehold on your dreams, and invite unexplored ideas into your understanding.

Using the Same Belief Pattern to Obtain a Different Life is Insane

How do you get something *different* using what is the *same*? That would be like using the same state map you used to drive to California to get to New York. Or it would be like trying to use an old sewing pattern that was cut perfectly for a short summer skirt to make a long winter coat.

This very moment is the product of yesterday's thinking, but you can change your mind right now about anything and do something different. As Sarah Ban Breathnach tells us:

Many of us unconsciously create dramas in our minds, expecting the worst from a situation only to have our expectations become a self-fufilling prophecy. Inadvertently, we become authors of our own misfortune. And so we struggle from day to day, crisis to crisis, bruised and battered by circumstances without realizing that we always have a choice. But what if you learned how to stop the dramas and started to trust the flow of life...? What if you began to expect the best from any situation? For many of us this is such a radical departure from the way we have been behaving that it seems unbelievable. Yet it is possible. Suspend your disbelief. Take a leap of faith. After all, what have you got to lose but misery and lack?

Most People Subconsciously Embrace Lack

They don't work on themselves; they don't seek to move beyond a certain plateau. They've tapered off and grown accustomed to doing just enough to survive. They've gotten fed up and have no interest in rediscovering enthusiasm.

It's necessary to trust yourself enough to take on new chances. Please understand that progress requires risk-taking. As Frederick Wilcox stated, "You can't steal second base and keep your foot on first."

Many People are Disenchanted with Life

How did we get limited? Where did this business of strapping down our potential come from? I believe all of us were visionaries at one time or another—most likely when we were children. But through the years, some people have allowed others to talk them out of dreaming. Now they're just enduring and surviving life rather than celebrating and enjoying it.

At some point, as a result of being exposed to negativity, you may have withdrawn your creative energy. Others may have convinced you that daydreaming is useless, silly and immature. Have you ever shared what you thought was a good idea with a friend, only to receive a train of negative feedback that left you doubting yourself? After repeatedly hearing that,"You can't do it"from well meaning parents, peers, siblings, co-workers, significant others and even strangers in passing, doubt often becomes a deep falsified reality for us. Options then appear to be void and choices seem gone. Consequently, this is when people learn to adapt to living average.

They may mean well, but folks who haven't realized their own dreams aren't the best sources for advice about yours. As you're aware, I was a product of an upbringing in which all of my caretakers had eyesight, but no one had vision for my life. I have used this as evidence that you can't be discouraged by another person's inability to see your specialness. Quite often, they're so preoccupied with their own injustices, burdens, and bad luck that there's no room to hope for you. Elbert Hubbard said, "There is something that is much more scarce, something rarer than ability. It's the ability to recognize ability."

Narrow Perceptions

Most of the time, people aren't trying to harm you with their closed minded negativity. It's just that they won't be able to see a blazing fire at the end of your tunnel, when they can't even imagine as much as a firefly at the end of theirs. People have their own demons they can't beat, bills coming they can't meet and people calling they can't greet. What emotional support could they possibly offer you?

Instead of pouring, selling or pleading your dream on people who can't see your vision, make it your personal quest and use your energy to just do it.

Your dreams are sacred; don't toss them about carelessly, leaving them vulnerable to people who are skeptical, bitter or jealous. You don't need an approval committee. Become empowered by knowing it isn't necessary that people see your potential. One thing is for sure, no one can dispute tangible facts. What is—is. Once you have accomplished your goal or goals, everything will become clear to others, but for now go on about the business of success. Who knows, you may even inspire doubters along the way. But through it all, be sure to refrain from taking on other people's limitations as your own.

Australian millionaire, Peter Daniels, had been told by an elementary school teacher he was a bad boy who would never amount to anything. Prior to becoming successful, he lived inside of this label of defeat that had been placed on him, but one day he got a wake-up call that changed both his opinion about himself and his life. He later wrote a book entitled, *Miss Phillips, You Were Wrong.*

So don't live your life through the eyes of disappointed people. They tend to be tapped out, stressed out, burned out, wigged out with bunches more to complain about. Their negative influences will make you tired before you get started. Trust me on this; no one who is working to realize their dream will tell you that you can't realize yours. With this in mind, go and reclaim your gifts.

What's Possible?

It's absolutely impossible for anyone to see everything that is available for your life. The combinations of possibility for you are infinite. No human being can accurately predict how your story will end. You can do anything! It's not possible to comprehend all you're capable of because it's far more than mortally imaginable! So don't let anyone try.

We have established that it's likely you've been misled by people who weren't qualified to share their wit and wisdom on success. Now you owe it to yourself to dismiss the negative nonsense. Decide to see more for your life right now! Simply think big. This will help expand your thinking beyond your current limitations.

S - t - r - e - t - c - h your ability to see more for your life than what is apparently available. When you do what you've always done, you'll get what you've always gotten. So we have to invite new information into our knowledge bank.

Learn more about yourself, other people, your field, your industry, this world and your contribution to it. You can't be what you can't see, so look beyond what's apparent.

Seeing the Possibility

If someone were to give you one apple, what could you do with it?

101

You could make a snack or perhaps give it to a co-worker who missed lunch. But how much more potential does this one apple have if we looked beyond the obvious? While most people see only one apple, I invite you to see something else with me. Every apple has ten seeds, and you can see them if you cut the fruit width wise. Imagine if you planted just one of the seeds. You would begin growing an entire apple tree!

I know it may be necessary to do some grafting for cross fertilization purposes, but the traditional planting procedure begins the way Johnny Appleseed did it, with a single small seed. If you planted all ten seeds, you would grow ten trees. Now you have an entire apple orchard. Who knows how many new apples per tree you'll grow—each one containing ten more seeds! Consider for a bit just how many needs you could fill with your expanding orchard.

There is a market for not only the fruit itself, but apple pie, apple butter, apple turnovers, apple sauce, apple cider, apple juice, apple vinegar and the list goes on!

What about the many possible uses of the wood from the trunks of your apple trees? There are log cabins, firewood, paper, and that list goes on!

Bees are one of the elements necessary for achieving a successful orchard. They are vital to the pollination of your trees, and with bees come honey. How lucrative are the many uses of honey?

If we can envision the potential for just one apple, and we didn't even scratch the surface, what more of the possibilities for human life—*your* life!

After seeing more for yourself, take inventory of your strengths and weaknesses. Figure out what you have to work on and strengthen your weak areas by spending time and money on your personal growth and development.

The average American reads only one book and spends less than ten dollars a year raising their consciousness. We spend more than that on pizza! If you read only one book a month in your area of expertise or desired field, you would have a significant competitive edge over most people in the entire country.

So be willing to engage in continuous learning. Do more of what you are doing right now. Read. If you don't like to read, listen to audio books, take classes or workshops, attend seminars, watch motivational videos and listen to cassettes and cd's that move you to action! Come early, stay late and burn the midnight oil to increase your understanding. You must expand your current mentality to get beyond where you are. Make a deliberate effort to clear space for a new level of consciousness.

Practice Daydreaming

Use your imagination to envision your success. The power of visualization is profound. You'll only be as successful as you can imagine. Your imagining capabilities help set the tone for your reality. Basically, if you think victory you live victoriously. How successful are the Kodak moments in your mind for your life? The extent of your imagination will be the extent of your success.

Right now envision an ink pen. It's pretty clear, right? Practice seeing your dreams as distinct as you would a writing tool or any other simple object, and you will get better at seeing and reaching your goals.

See your goals in living color, much like you would a motion picture. This movie is for you, by you and starring you. This is your movie! You are brilliant and look stunning! See being more than a survivor, more than successful. See yourself being significant! What are you doing, wearing, saying? Who do you see? What are you hearing? And who is hearing you? See yourself attracting positive people who mean you well and who are supporting your plight. See yourself transcending old thoughts of doubt and achieving success. See yourself starting that business, going back to school, building your ministry or reaching whatever your personal goal.

Finally, actively participate in your healing. On the next page is an exercise that I call an "Erase and Replenish Statement." Record this statement on audio in your own voice. Listen to it daily as you also read along with the recording. This will help clear you of self-limiting beliefs and replace them with thoughts that support growth and achievement.

Erase & Replenish Statement

I was afraid of change. I am not afraid anymore. Change comes naturally for me. I welcome this opportunity to start fresh. I am excited about the life that is being transformed into the life I want. The life that I have and the life I want are one. I am grateful for my new happiness. I forgive myself for all the past choices I've made that have not served me well. I now know better and I will do better.

Even when I make mistakes, I will become wiser from them and continue to forgive myself. I forgive others for speaking and modeling negativity in my life. None of that is about me, and I will not take it personally. I will safeguard my precious ears and mind from messages and words that do not support thoughts of abundance.

I can easily filter out toxic language and feast on what is positive. I am confident in what I am doing. I trust myself completely. Others may not see my vision. But I am sure my dream is real. My faith is sufficient. And with the help of God, I can do anything I make up my mind to do.

Please don't underestimate the affects this statement can have on your life. Right now it may not seem earth-shaking, but it works. Remember, complicated problems usually have simple solutions.

Sometimes Motivation Alone Can't Pull Off Our Blinders

When we feel trapped, it's very real. When your back is up against a wall and you can't think of anything positive you've ever heard or read, by all means, feel free to deliver into the hands of God things known or unknown that are blocking your view. Ask that He correct any misconceptions tainting your thought pattern and causing you to make poor choices.

Now girded with a made up mind, a new commitment to yourself, the realization that others may have spoon fed you negativity, and with the eagerness to live your best life, you may be saying,

"Asha I'm ready to move to the next level and really do this." And to you I say, *"Let's go!"*

CHAPTER 5

The Key to Dealing with Difficult People

Difficult individuals are at the bank, at work, the grocery store, the mall, school...all over. And no matter how smart you get or how long you live, you will have to deal with them. So let's get to it!

First, we must ask ourselves why we experience certain people as being difficult to begin with. The answer to this will be relevant to building your strategy.

Generally speaking, we expect more of people than what we should. We insist they do better, and we bang our heads against walls trying to get them to see it the "right" way—our way. When they fail to meet our expectations, we label them "difficult." We keep at them because we hope something we say or do will wake them up. We all say we know we can't change anyone, but harnessed with hope, we still try. Only in this context will I say to you, give up hope."Blessed is the one who expects nothing for they shall never be disappointed!"

Why shouldn't we expect anything from people? Aren't there universal principles or just basic manners that everyone should live by?

Perhaps, perhaps not. It really doesn't matter one way or the other because you will never get everyone to agree to the same standards of living. So, it's best to take people where they are realistically—not where they should be ideally.

Why People Are Difficult

Low self-esteem is an epidemic. The lack of self-esteem in our society is frightening. It's a treacherous vice grip that costs emotional, financial, spiritual and physiological vitality for many people.

Select any disastrous situation in our society. As you pull back the layers of that particular situation, notice that most of the time the root of the problem is the same—somebody didn't love himself enough. When we don't love ourselves enough we can't love anybody else; when we can't love anybody else anything goes! This is where we begin to see problems in droves.

The problems include everything from personal misery to poverty, racism, robbery, suicide, murder, and war.

Consider Columbine. Teenage boys who love themselves don't see killing as an option.

Consider cult experiences. People who have feelings of worthiness don't need to lead others to destruction; and people who love themselves don't choose to follow them.

Consider difficult people. It doesn't matter what type of difficult person you encounter: nosy, know-it-all, manipulative, emotional bullies...you name it, the root of the problem is always the same—low self-esteem.

If you are at least twenty years old, you have seen each type before. You are what I call a "professional lifer" which means you are an expert at identifying the various behaviors of people. You have seen it before on someone, somewhere.

Routinely recognizing these behaviors will allow you to prepare yourself for dealing with them when they come. The more you practice, the better you'll get. After some time, difficult people will virtually not affect you.

Where Is the Love?

People aren't born difficult. As children most were optimistic, fearless and innocent.

So what happened?

Life happened, and some people weren't emotionally equipped to deal with challenges in a healthy manner. So, they started taking on the masks of nosy, bully, complaining, etc. They became "difficult."

Difficult isn't who they really are. They really are people of magnificence, but they don't know that, and they are doing the best they can at surviving behind these masks.

To deal with anyone's negative behavior affectively, you must pull back the masks in search of their innocence.

You can do this with anyone who is difficult. Let's take "nosy" for instance. What is behind the mask?

Nosy people are in your desk, your business, your conversations, your emails...Why?

If nosy could reach the depths of their own pain, they might answer like this:

"I am nosy because I think things are going on behind my back. And I have to play private eye to stay in the know. I don't believe people are being honest with me or keeping me in the loop; they really don't like me, so in order to be a part of the happenings, I have to obnoxiously make my presence known. I do this because I know I'm not interesting, fascinating or lovable enough for people to involve me in their lives willingly.

"Another reason I'm in your business is because I need your information for gossiping purposes. I know gossiping is wrong,

but it helps me feel close to people, and makes me feel better to know that someone in the world is feeling just as miserable as I am.

"Knowing the 'scoop.'is all that I have to take pride in. I don't know what else to talk about. The few people who do talk to me only do so because they think I know stuff about everybody's life. I guess what I'm saying is, I kinda use gossip to barter for people's attention—which I'm unworthy of otherwise. I want to have meaningful relationships, and I want to be loved; I just don't know how. So here I stand, preoccupying myself with your choices and judging every aspect of your life because doing so keeps me from having to contend with the emptiness in my own."

Pulling back the masks like this will be effective for any difficult personality type you encounter, even emotional bullies. Behind the mask of the bully you might find this voice:

"I am not a softy; I'm tough! Being nice to people doesn't pay. I used to be nice, but I always got hurt or was made a fool of. But no more! I will tell you where to get off, and I won't care how you feel about it. I really don't want to be this way, but nobody cares about me, so I have to protect myself.

"I don't know how else to be. Being mean makes me feel powerful in a world that never showed me any love. I don't know how to handle situations without being rude. Life has shown me that if I'm not aggressive I will get eaten alive, and I just can't seem to see things any other way, no matter how hard I try.

"I'm loud because I'm trying to talk over the pain that I am feeling. I'm angry about so many things that I can't even identify what they are anymore. I compensate for my feelings of inadequacy by dominating other people and making them feel small. I don't have any control in my own life, so the only thing I know to do is try and control yours."

From this you can see where the masks are just that—masks. People are basically good, but often portray themselves otherwise because they are injured and not convinced of their own goodness.

You might be thinking, *"So what am I supposed to do about that? We all have problems. You don't get to take your personal matters out on other people simply because you aren't clued into your own goodness!"*

Having compassion for them is not about them as much as it is about you. There are tremendous benefits for you when you empathize with others. Compassion safeguards you. Remember, "you reap what you sow."

Giving Others a Break

Giving other people a break when they are behaving the only way they know how inherently boomerangs compassion back into your life.

Many people aren't shown mercy when they make mistakes. So they subconsciously don't give anyone else a break. Instead, they pounce on every opportunity to magnify other people's errors. When others mess up, for once, it wasn't them, and they have to let the world know!

But if you are generous and free with forgiving others, it will naturally build you a shield of protection when you need it most.

If you can't seem to muster up enough room in your heart to deal with difficult people lovingly, I suggest that a significant ingredient is missing from your life. This particular ingredient is the best defense for dealing with difficult people, and oddly enough, it is a brief one sentence concept.

I'm not talking about something that helps you ignore

difficult people or pretend what they say or do doesn't bother you. I'm saying you won't be moved by them because this concept will make you absolutely immune to any person you encounter who is hard to get along with! This one ingredient can make it impossible for anyone to disappoint you ever again.

What is this powerful theory that is so simple that it can be put into one sentence?

The ultimate key to dealing with difficult people is to build your own self-esteem!

This may not jump off the page at you as being that profound—at first glance. We certainly have heard a lot about self-esteem. People have been talking about the need for it and its benefits for years, and still the lack of it is rampant. But that has to change in your life before you can be successful.

Poor Self-esteem is the Source of Personal Pain

When you lack self-esteem, all the good advice anybody ever gives you, including mine, will not help you solve your problems. But when you are grounded in self-worth, you realize you can cope with anything and anybody. When you have self-esteem is high and you know how to maintain it, you participate in life in such a way that produces miracles!

When you feel good about yourself all the time, you attract both the people and the events into your life that empower and position you for opportunities most people never dream possible.

Although many have self-esteem, most people don't. The ones who don't can't accept every aspect of themselves without feeling overwhelmed by their weaknesses. Meanwhile they fail to recognize their strengths.

Now I'm asking you to recognize, and celebrate the

sacred, well deserving, magnificent being you are.

"That's all fine Asha, but what does my self-esteem have to do with other people's behavior?"

Simple. Loving *yourself* unconditionally changes how *you* perceive yourself, and that changes how *you* come to the table of life. How you perceive yourself and participate in life determines how others will receive and treat you, everywhere you go.

Anybody Can Be Insecure

You don't have to be a psychopath, a criminal or even the product of a dysfunctional home to experience the affects of insecurity. Average hardworking, well-meaning, tax-paying, law abiding individuals who want to achieve success have to be mindful of the subtle ways in which feelings of unworthiness can creep in.

They can show up in the hesitation to except a compliment or in shunning attention for your achievements.

Have you ever given someone a compliment and they disowned it? You may have said, "Your hair looks very nice." They frown and gesture away your words as they simultaneously say, "Oh, what are you talking about? it looks awful; it needs to be done!" At that point, you don't know what to say. You almost feel a need to apologize for having said anything at all.

There are many more not-so-obvious indications of a person with a breach of love for themselves, including: sinking into depression; over-eating, lying, smoking, hoarding money, "cheating," engaging in unlawful activity, distrusting, manipulating, accumulating clutter, being a perfectionist, acting irresponsibly, refusing to be accountable for mistakes, blaming others, growing violent, or gambling excessively. This lack of self-love also underlies behavior that is argumentative, dishonest, sexist, irresponsible, fearful cynical, competitive, withdrawn, jealous or just plain mean.

Sound like anybody you? Some symptoms may remind you of your own life, and that's okay. We are all human. That is what this growth thing is about—recognizing your needs and doing something about them.

You may have noticed that I say *symptom* of low self-esteem as though it were a disease. Again, low self-esteem, like a disease, is a full fledged epidemic! You might be thinking, it must not be that bad with so many people doing some of the things mentioned.

Please don't be misled by the popularity of these behaviors. Debt, worry, stress and unfulfillment are popular too! But who wants that?

How Did We Get Here?

Mostly, low self-esteem is the result of what we were programmed to believe as children. Children are impressionable and need approval. If you didn't feel valued, praised, rewarded, celebrated, protected, welcomed, trusted, nurtured, respected, worthy, important, special, talented, smart, capable, beautiful and lovable as a child, it took a toll on how you responded to life as an adult. And it's never something that you can hide. Compromised self-esteem always shows up somewhere in our lives. When you are not easily forgiven for your mistakes as a child, you become a non-forgiving and judgmental adult.

So be fair with yourself. How you do that is by first finding out what is beneath it all. What bothers you and why? At the root of your feelings will be what holds you back from prosperity. So take this exercise seriously. Give skin to your emotions by acknowledging them. Do you have feelings of guilt, anger, resentment? If so, don't try to pretend everything is fine. Own all of your thoughts and dispositions. Then give yourself permission to feel them. When we are detached from our own emotions, we get lost in trying to cover our pain. That's pure torture, much like holding absolutely still and suppressing a scream while your foot is stuck under a truck!

Suppressing ourselves is how we become disconnected from ourselves. Your feelings are valid whatever they are. If it hurts, allow it. Then derive a plan for handling the pain from its fountainhead.

We must be brave enough to examine ourselves as individuals and set our own standards of normalcy and excellence. Live life on your own terms; but first love yourself enough to know you deserve to.

Do I think everyone has low self-esteem? No, but I believe everyone has areas of insecurity on some level. It is possible to love yourself immensely and still have vulnerable spots that could stand improvement. We all must be willing to search those areas out and commit to doing the work of healing. We are always a work in progress. The goal is to evolve more and more each day. This will enable you to make healthier choices for your life.

What Do You See?

What is your primary perception of yourself? Are you in love with you? Do you adore who you are? Can you smile in the mirror? Do you like what you see, even on a "bad hair day"? Are you happy to see yourself in the morning? Many people are afraid they will sound conceited, so they go all the way to the other end of the continuum by having little or no esteem at all.

Join Asha's VIP Club FREE at www.ashatyson.com for further support

Much of how you see yourself is based on the comments and actions of the caretakers you had in your earliest years. But you have to consider that they may not have been capable of teaching you how to appreciate yourself.

They could only see for you what they had seen in themselves. Your caretakers may not have been shown how to love themselves, and now it's sadly your inheritance. Self-doubt, self-dislike and distrust has a contagious recycling affect. That's why it is important to recognize any emotional cracks and choose to fill your gaps with love if you are going to be a parent.

It isn't coincidental that teenage pregnancies are often repeated within a family, nor that children who had parents who accepted verbal and emotional abuse from a companion often choose the same kind of relationships. It is important that parents guard against perpetuating self-lovelessness in child raising.

Generally, parents have goals of giving their children better lives than what they had. But where do parents learn how to do that? We are naturally creatures of habit, who can only do what we know even when it isn't necessarily the best thing. If parents don't demonstrate what it *looks* like to have self-love, how will a child learn to be an example for their own children and so on? If unworthiness is maintained generation after generation, we end up with an entire society that is emotionally sick. Someone once said, "Children learn what they live." It is my belief that children learn what *you* live.

I was keynoting a conference where a woman later shared that her son, who was eight years old, showed her how important her actions were as a parent.

His teacher began recognizing some irrational behavior. He was smart and well adjusted usually, but something started happening to him every day approximately ten minutes before it was time to go home. Whenever the teacher announced to the class, "Class begin to gather your things; it's almost time to go home," he went into a frenzy and became anxious! He rushed around fumbling his belongings. Calm was nowhere to be found. This kid was having a panic attack!

The teacher decided to speak with his mother one afternoon when she picked him up from school. She explained the situation and expressed her concern: "This is the only time of the day I've ever witnessed him do anything like this."

That evening the mother, who was very nurturing and attentive to her only child, could not imagine why he rushed around as though someone had made a bomb threat. She pondered all night, and then it came to her.

Every morning, before she dropped him off at school before jetting herself to work, they were always in a hurry. He had watched her rat race around, nervously trying to get out of the house so often that it had become routine—a way of life. For him, this was normal and appropriate.

Her son had gotten a distinct message from *watching* his mother that in life when it's time to go, everyone should flip out!

And so you see, parents must examine their behaviors while in the presence of impressionable minds. Children are watching in the grocery store when you exhibit frustration and annoyance with the cashier, and they learn impatience. They are watching how you react when the dry cleaners doesn't have your clothes ready on time. They are monitoring your social skills when you laugh with your friends then talk about them later behind their backs. They seek to find what angers you in this world, what makes you smile, and what makes you cry. Care givers are like deity in the eyes of little people, and even what you don't say gets heard.

The Good News!

You are born again anytime you go into a situation and consciously leave the perceptions of the past behind. You can do this in any given second you choose! You can reclaim your self-worth by revisiting your own innocence and healing your past. Even if you did not have a tragic childhood, there is still work to be done. There is always room for improvement. There is always another level available to explore.

Emotional wounds can be developed in the most inconspicuous ways during the course of life. So do some self assessing and get in touch with your value. Doing so can significantly improve the quality of your life; not doing it will compromise your happiness and can cost you money!

Yes, money.

Consider this: A person becomes depressed about one thing or another. She takes her charge card and goes on a radical shopping spree. The bill comes, and she doesn't have the money to pay it. Now she's depressed about that too. Her private storm continues; the bills are piling up and the depression mounts. The original pain still exists because she never confronted the issues surrounding it. Shopping may have soothed her temporarily, but afterwards the money is gone.

How we handle, manage, save and spend our dollars is in direct proportion to how we manage our emotions, and this can be very unhealthy.

Why?

When we have feelings of worthlessness that go unrelieved, we only go deeper in depression and deeper in debt.

The failure to recognize your worth and participate in self development is the same as blatantly refusing to live successfully. We must take care of ourselves thoroughly. We don't readily do that. Often, we feel guilty when we try to steal moments of peace for ourselves. Instead of indulging fully, some people are thinking about all the other projects and chores they should be doing. They live from the "someday" philosophy.

"Someday, after the kids are gone, when the holidays are over, after I get a better job, when I have more money, I'll do it someday." Someday can be eternal. As the saying goes, "Life is what passes us by while we are planning to live." So we must have a sense of urgency about loving ourselves.

Also, *how* we love ourselves matters. Pedicures, manicures, precise hair and such are fine. Wearing nice clothing, keeping an immaculate home, and looking pulled together helps to show the world you are intending to be "quality people." This is fine, but it has its place. Make no mistake; these things are cosmetic and are no true indications of true success. They are just props, and dressing up is the easy part. The real *work* is in becoming internally whole.

You'll Know the Work Is Working

You may not see your emotional growth right away, but you'll know it's there when the same old stuff doesn't affect you the same way it used to.

When you are in the presence of that one person who always tries to make you look bad, they won't have the same effect on you. Offense won't even resonate in your body.

The work will be evident when someone's approval or disapproval doesn't confuse you once you've made your final decision. You will feel the work when it is easier to say "no" to others without feeling guilty. You will know the work is affecting you when you are content with yourself in uninterrupted silence. You will be able to sit home alone for an evening with no music, books, television, phone or anything—just the sound of your eyelashes growing. We don't often like the interior discipline that comes with being still by ourselves.

If you find being alone with yourself exceptionally difficult, be willing to evaluate why. If you are incapable of spending an evening alone with you, why should someone else want to?

It is a dangerous reality that if you don't fall in love with yourself you will look outside for it. When you look externally for love, acceptance and approval, you run the risk of being misinformed, misled and heartbroken. Desperately looking for love in all the wrong faces will just cost you more of your own self worth. Relationships based on starvation will always be impoverished. As long as a person lacks self-love, they will attract people who make them even more dependent. And to be successful and free, we must be emotionally self-sufficient. When you can live these truths you will know the soulwork is working.

Self-love or Just Selfish?

Self-love is often mistakenly perceived as selfishness, but who can you help if you are on empty? Besides being selfish means to have little or no concern for others. You can have regard for your own interests and welfare while holding respect for others, but you can't have genuine concern for others when you have no regard for yourself. Many people try to please others, fit in and be accepted, but if you have allowed yourself to be pushed or pulled out of emotional shape just to be liked, you are not bringing one hundred percent of yourself to the table!

Self-love or confidence is not conceit or vanity, although it may appear to be for others looking on who aren't loving themselves enough. Conceit is an exaggeration of ones accomplishments. It's loaded with whimsy that is not founded on much truth. Conceited people have low self-esteem, which is why they find it necessary to blow their own horn. Confident people are firmly convinced that they are capable. They trust themselves, and their abilities are proven to be solid and founded on truth.

Your Self-esteem Building Action Plan

You may have noticed that I frequently mention "the work." This simply means the consistent action that you take daily to improve yourself—your life. For instance, if you currently keep a gratitude journal, that is a soulwork act. If you consciously take time to do nothing but sit with yourself for fifteen minutes a day, that is a soulwork act. If you deliberately engage in self-esteem building exercises with tapes or workbooks, that is a soulwork act.

If you have not begun a self-esteem building action plan, begin one immediately. Here is a good place to start or to supplement your existing plan:

Get a box, bag, basket, drawer or whatever container works for you. Life is very personal. Customize it for your individual needs. I prefer using a ring binder filled with plain paper. With this, you are going to deliberately engage in building your self worth.

Keep inventory of your small victories. Write them down. When I was in college, I had a friend who would contemplate her research paper after completing it. She would hold it and balance it in her hands minute or two, enjoying the weight of it as she danced. In that moment, this one accomplishment represented dedication, discipline and competence, which she chose to isolate and celebrate.

It may sound strange, but trying to do what seems logical or "normal" may not be what serves *your* life. If romping around the house with a finished project in your hand builds your self-esteem and unleashes more of your creative energy, who cares how silly it looks?

We don't often take the time to celebrate our daily accomplishments. We get too busy moving on to the next thing and the next one and the next one—much like swinging from limb to limb in a jungle. When life becomes a chore rather than a joy, something has to be adjusted. Review your victory journal frequently. You will be surprised at how it renews your spirit.

Next, make a list of statements you want to affirm and demonstrate in your life about who you are. Your statements can include anything from "I am a worthwhile person" to "I am accepted, I am secure, I am significant because I am here." Affirmations are powerful and effective. Don't underestimate the impact they can have on your life.

If you are blessed to still have a parent who would be willing to record these things about you that would be helpful. But it isn't necessary. You can do this yourself. Affirmations work just as well when it is your own voice.

Whatever you do, don't get stopped. Through these affirmations, you are developing some good press about yourself. What are some of your best compliments? What about you do you find interesting, lovable, endearing, admirable, powerful, unique, special? It is okay to be superficial in this exercise. It all counts; there is no harm in acknowledging what is so. If you have perfect teeth or are simply drop-dead gorgeous, then own it. It's yours!

Create some self-esteem vitamins! Get a large empty aspirin bottle and fill it with compliments to yourself on small pieces of paper. Design these statements specifically for you. Each morning, read one as if you were taking a vitamin. Now don't laugh. It may be corny, but it works.

Monitor your own self-talk. Many times our worst enemy comes from within. Do you have a tone of cynicism, or apathy? Pay close attention to the messages you tell yourself throughout the day. Make sure they are synonymous with prosperity. If not, change them. Be brave enough to own how you might be creating self sabotage through your own language.

Learn a new skill, take up journaling, play a sport, accept a new challenge, and rediscover your childlike qualities. Color, play jacks, buy race cars or a train set, mold something with clay, make and throw water balloons, sponsor a Barbie doll pizza party for your daughter and her friends. If you don't have a little girl, borrow one. Play twister with your own friends. Find some bumper cars. Enjoy some "nonsense" for a change. We become so mature that at times we mock the very essence of what it means to be happy. Being reasonable can confuse you.

Write short stories, sketch, design your own clothing line, take karate. Spoil yourself. Play miniature golf, go bowling, indulge in a bubble bath with scented candles. Get good at doing absolutely nothing—guilt-free. You deserve to be loving and gentle with yourself. Isn't it time? If not now, when?

You might be thinking: *Speaking of time, I don't have any!*

I am not suggesting you *fit* happiness in along with everything else you're doing. Believe you me I understand the demands of a hectic schedule. I am suggesting you scratch something that is no longer serving you and integrate joy instead! When you are changing your life, the same things you started with on your plate should not be the same things there after the change. Change means just that—change! Evaluate how you are doing things; then alter and delete what just ain't working.

Don't Fix What's not Broken

Change for the sake of change doesn't make anymore sense than doing the same nonproductive stuff over and over again. Be willing to examine whether or not this current disposition of your life is still working well for you, that is to say, if it ever worked at all. If you find that some or all of the way you live now is not pleasing to you, dare to be different. Self-love has to be a nonnegotiable priority, not something you feel is jamming up your schedule. Self-love becomes your schedule if you don't have it, because nothing else you do will substantiate without it.

Nothing you create will matter or last if it isn't built on a solid foundation of knowing you are worthy and always have been. These are known facts. Parents who love themselves are better parents. Employers, employees, husbands, wives, significant others, sisters, brothers, teachers, lawyers, business people, bus drivers, fast food crews and every person you've ever met are better individuals when they love themselves from the inside out. So we know that to be truly successful you must value your self-esteem building action plan as a mandatory requirement—not an option.

You Want to Be Free?

Get up close and personal with yourself, heal the emotional wounds of the past that are often carried into the choices made in life, repair your broken heart, rejuvenate enthusiasm, and understand your feelings by asking yourself tough questions. Validate your feelings. Fill what is void, strengthen what is weak, pamper what has been neglected and soothe what's sore. Fall in love with yourself, indulge and emerge solely in unconditional self-acceptance. Fast, pray, give professional counseling a try, get determined to improve, and get persistent about living a first rate life.

It is your reward for doing this soulwork that renders loving relationships, a healthy body, meaningful work and fat bank accounts! Don't miss out on yours simply because you never got around to appreciating and adoring the one person you will spend the rest of your life with—you.

CHAPTER 6

How to Cope with Difficult Circumstances

The number one way to cope with difficult circumstances is to take responsibility for your part in them.

Take personal responsibility for your entire life—every aspect of it. Own up to everything you have or don't have. To be successful, we must be accountable for our choices, good or bad. People who find it toughest to cope are usually the ones who have subconsciously elected to be victims of their circumstances.

These victims have surrendered their power. Everything unfortunate that's happened to them was and is always someone else's fault. Living as a victim is almost as much of an epidemic as the emotional sickness that created it—low self- esteem. If we're insecure with ourselves, we won't be able to separate our mistakes from who we are.

We are lovable, capable, worthy individuals, and making mistakes doesn't change that. That is why it's unnecessary to try to hide your imperfections.

Imperfections remind me of a new leather coat or bag. When the material is genuine, there is usually a tag attached to the item that says something:

"This article has been authentically crafted. You may

notice some disruptions in the material. However, these are not defects. They are bites, stretch marks and scratches that are indigenous of the leather."And so it is with us.

We are Perfect Inside of Our Imperfections

Making mistakes is indigenous to the human condition. In other words, it's okay to "blow it, goof or make a mess of things." Just have enough integrity to clean it up, offer remorse and extend full restitution. This is what it means to be accountable for your actions.

Instead of owning their mistakes, most people have no accountability. Instead, they waste energy justifying their shortcomings and trying to avoid looking bad. In the long run, it is this lack of accountability that makes life hard.

Many folks are full of never ending excuses as to why they aren't living the lives of their dreams, and by now I know you've heard every excuse possible...

They would have, should have and could have if only they had reliable transportation; if the economy wasn't in a recession; if they could get work; if their husband had believed in them; if the children weren't a challenge; if they had a companion; if they could get a loan; if Charlie had done his part; if they had more time; if their mother had loved them as much as their brother; if they hadn't believed in someone who betrayed them; if they hadn't been rejected so many times; if their boss had a clue; if they hadn't been held back; if they hadn't been ridiculed; if they had the opportunity to go to college; if they looked like Jennifer Lopez; if they had parents; if they weren't teased; if they hadn't been disappointed so often; if the baby's daddy would do his part; if they were given a raise; if they were appreciated at work; if they were smarter; if somebody had helped them; if they had been the Australian Outback Survivor; if they had been encouraged; if they had been a man, if they had been black; if they had been a woman; if they had been white; if they had Oprah's money; if they weren't so busy; if they had some support; if they had a father in the home; if they had a home; if they knew their real parents; if they had somebody to exercise with; if they could get on their feet; if she would stop drinking; if he would get a job; if they hadn't lost a parent at a young age; if the supervisor liked them; if they knew somebody; if this never happened; if that never happened; and if they had known what they know now...they would be successful!

Most people don't want to own their participation in being broke, lonely or unfulfilled. They don't realize that being irresponsible for our own lives in every aspect cripples growth. Excuse-making seems to flow effortlessly from the mouths of most, but it costs in more ways than we can imagine.

Practicing helplessness can debilitate even the sharpest people, so be on the lookout for this in your life. Individuals who whine and complain do so to distract themselves and others from seeing the real reasons why they don't achieve. But we don't want to be excuse-making, buck-passing defense masters. Professional justifiers don't accomplish anything. This kind of self-piracy is dangerous because the more people do it, the better they get at it.

Why it's Easy for Us to Fall into Self-Destruction

There are payoffs for playing the victim in our society. If victims can convince enough somebodies that they don't have what it takes to make it, of course, by no fault of their own, people will give them pity, leniency, and resources. Don't look to victims to take the rap for their lives falling apart.

Their story is always the same. Once upon a time, they were ready, willing and able to be successful. Then one day a villain from planet "eat the powerless" threw a road block in their path. Now they can't move, and they can prove it! They say they were average, honest, hard-working people who didn't want much. Then something or someone came along and held them back. Since then, they have been dedicated to protesting success. People are their enemies and the world is their battleground. Now they have no choice but to live unhappily ever after. The End.

Before long, victims don't even have to defend themselves. Loved ones argue their cases for them, pave the way and even foot their bills. This usually enables the victim and makes the big bad world seem all the more real. Victim supporters say things like, "She could if...; he would do so much better if...; he tried but...; if somebody would just motivate her, she would..."

Why would anybody let a volunteer victim use them and ride on their compassion?

The answer is couched inside of the esteem issues we discussed earlier. Some people with personal insecurities need to be needed so badly that they allow their generosity to be abused. These people are self-appointed *saviors* in order to make their own lives more meaningful. If they weren't fixing, changing and repairing someone else, what would give their lives meaning?

The danger of being a savior is that your priorities get scrambled, and unless you close your 24-hour personal rescue mission, you will never get around to living your own best life.

More Good News!

Victims are free, the bad news is they don't know it. The worst news is they don't even know that they don't know. They are free to choose, decide, think, create, change, move and grow, but being free and not having a clue is like living trapped in a cold, dark, dungeon—hungry and sick for several years. At one point, people stopped by and offered help, but the prisoner-victim convinced potential helpers that the situation was hopeless. Instead, these victims stay stuck and complain. Meanwhile, they never recognize that the lock on the door is and always has been made of cotton!

You Are Absolutely Free to Redesign Your Life!

Regardless of how out of control or emotionally impaired you may have felt, you can and will have to save yourself. Find the courage to dig deep within the crevices of your own soul and target the source of your pain. Do you feel someone owes you? Do you feel everyone owes you? If so, release the anger and use that energy to execute a new game plan for your life. It's impossible to have a successful recovery stuck inside of who you think failed, deserted or stopped you.

We've all experienced misfortune. Many of us have been exposed to some of the most humiliating and unimaginable situations, but you aren't what has happened to you. You are not the embodiment of tragedy. You may have lived through some victimizing circumstances, but never were you anybody's victim. So it's up to you to recognize your power and choose not to give it away.

If you are faulting your parents, your siblings, your boss, the institutions, the media, religion, your family, the system, the people at work, the hospitals, the neighbors, the schools, your ex, former employers, your in-laws, the administration, the clinics, the economy, the government, the politicians, the Internet, organized crime, disorganized crime, the rich, the poor, the good, the bad or the ugly, you will never find the abundance you so rightly deserve.

Sure, people could have been more accommodating along the way. They weren't. Now what do we do? You must give up being right about being "done to." You have to release the stronghold you have on being the "underdog." These rackets have not served you; let them go and make room for beliefs that will push you in the direction of your goals.

If you passionately believe you can't do anything to change your situation, you'll have no problem finding evidence to prove yourself right! No matter how many solutions are offered to help you get out of a dilemma, you will always have the same response — "yeah, but...yeah, but...yeah, but..."

If you allow yourself to obtain comfort in blaming external entities for your own lack, you become so busy defending your right to be incapable, you will have missed opportunity. Please be very careful that you're not in denial on this one. Some people have preached their "poor me" sermon so much, they now believe their message is gospel.

Being Victim Is Expensive

Living as a victim can and will cost you quality of life, and that includes money! Being *account*able for your choices is what helps to grow your account. You simply can't find financial opportunity when all you see are the wrongdoers in your life. Be brave enough to ask others around you what your walk and talk is about. Do people know your complaints by heart. Have you taught them so well they can recite your helplessness verbatim?

Become fully responsible for your life. Responsible people feel capable of owning all the consequences of their decisions. They are girded with integrity. They feel strong in who they are, and they know that making mistakes is perfectly okay. When you are a responsible individual, you need only recognize your error, learn from it and do better next time. This kind of freedom will enable you to see a latitude of possibilities for power, passion and profit in your life.

Victims can't see a million dollar idea if you poured it on them because they are consumed with explaining their helplessness. They are unequipped to move to resolution because they have spent too much time sharpening their defensive skills. And they are good at it! Resolving problems and being happy isn't as important to them as being right. So, although they are always *right*, they are never truly happy.

Take pride in your errors by claiming them and being available to rectify them. It is this kind of integrity that builds trust in both business and personal relationships. When people know you to be a person who tells the truth and comes to the table of your endeavors with clean hands, they'll give you respect, information, money or anything else you want, and rightfully they should.

Rising to the Challenge

Anyone who can rise to the challenge of giving and keeping their word ought to be rewarded greatly. If you find that it's not feasible to keep your first word, then be responsible enough to communicate the situation with people before rather than after the fact. Being accountable means seeing it through from start to finish, beginning to end. It means sticking around to own it all, your mistakes, your triumphs, your shortcomings, your victories—everything. Anybody can reap the perks of being the captain, but the real question is: are you willing to go down with the ship? Most people aren't going down with any ship. Instead, they scream,, "It's not my fault" or " It's not like I did it on purpose."

It's interesting to see how we bombard others with excuses about traffic, being trapped in meetings, losing track of time, dropping off children and the million other explanations we show up with when we're late. The reality is we're late. The best thing to do is acknowledge people for their patience, recognize the value of their time by ensuring them you got there as quickly as possible, and sincerely apologize; they are entitled to that. Why waste more time spouting a bunch of reasons that don't change the tardiness? Just be accountable for being late. If you're late, you're late. Period. Forgive yourself, ask for forgiveness and move on.

Time isn't the only place that a lack of responsibility shows up in our lives. Many of us have seen it even when loaning or borrowing money. I call it the dodge-chase game. It goes something like this:

Someone borrows money from a friend, and on the day they're to pay it back, the lender doesn't hear from them. Maybe two or three days later, the borrower calls with excuses and makes new arrangements to repay the loan, but the new arrangements don't happen and the lender subsequently doesn't hear from anybody. The lender then takes the initiative to call, but the borrower is conveniently never available. The lender feels dodged, and the chase is on!

Correspondence ceases altogether as the borrower avoids the lender. By the time they bump into each other, by mistake from the borrower's perspective, the borrower gets selective amnesia and acts as if money isn't due. The lender is too embarrassed to mention the loan. So everybody walks away to avoid confrontation. The borrower feels relieved and the lender feels deceived.

Sometimes the lender is brave enough to ask about the money, and the borrower insists the loan was paid back or they claim they had been trying or meaning to call. *Has the money come between friends?* No. It's never about the money itself. It has more to do with the lender's desire to be respected and appreciated for being there in a time of need. The lender feels duped by a borrower masquerading as a true friend. Not being paid back and having no idea if and when the borrower has any intention of paying, is what puts the discomfort in this scenario.

The borrower simply doesn't have the money, and doesn't know how to be responsible for the debt at this point. It does take a great deal of courage to face a creditor who is ready to be paid when you don't have the money, but it's the accountable borrower who will be a brave soul and *show up* anyhow.

After running for so long, the borrower stops caring what the lender thinks. Now the bridge is burned, and Judge Judy is called.

The highest act of accountability in a borrowing/lending situation is to pay the money back as originally agreed. If for some reason this does not happen, the borrower should put integrity back in place by hammering out a few options and communicating with the lender about when to expect the money. A payment plan might be necessary, but whatever the agreement, the borrower should stay in touch with the lender and keep every promise along the way. Lenders are usually very understanding when they can see genuine efforts.

If the borrower is having financial hardships, establishing and reestablishing agreements may go back and forth a few times, but with each conversation a payment should be made. This will demonstrate good faith. The important thing is to be convicted enough to handle the debt as a priority.

The borrower must be answerable until every dime is paid. The lender at no time should feel forgotten or ignored. The borrower should at no time disappear. In fact, the borrower should chase the lender until the debt is clear, not the other way around.

On a personal note, I find borrowing, lending, cosigning and engaging in any kind of financial contract with friends and family to be uncomfortable, so I don't do any of it anymore. It's a choice I made some time ago that works for my life and needs no explanation. When asked, "Why not?" I tell people that it's merely an "Asha thing."

If you decide that you don't mind borrowing and loaning money, do what is comfortable for you. Just be responsible to all parties involved, including yourself. Never borrow more than you can pay back, and never loan more than you can lose.

What It Means to Be Accountable to Others

Being a responsible or accountable individual is to own up to any and every aspect of your life—good, bad or indifferent. It means to be your word, be dependable, reliable, fair and honorable. Know when the ball is in your court, and blame no one for your choices. Make your apologies before the actual agreement has been breached. Pay for what you have used, taken or broken. Replace what you have disturbed. Know when it's your turn to make things right. Acknowledge when it's you who caused the harm, and be prepared to repair or replenish.

Where you have participated in offending another, remorsefully restore what has come undone. Always make things whole as tactfully and graciously as possible. When you are humble and responsible during the times you err, others won't find it necessary to burn you at the stake.

Being Accountable to Yourself

Be careful not to wrongfully diagnose your challenges. If you think your problem is someone else's fault, you will look to others for the solution. Since the solutions to your life are within you, the outward search will always be in vain. It would be like looking for your purse at your sister's house when it's actually at yours. No matter how strategic your search is, if you are looking in the wrong place for something, it's as good as not looking at all.

By now, we know that the average person faults others for their deficiencies and that the repercussions are dangerous. You simply can't properly steer your life from the back seat of the car. You must plant yourself in the driver's seat. If your life is not what you want it be, it's your responsibility to fix it.

Blaming Others Is an Illusion

To really improve your life, you have to be willing to be responsible for your part in creating the state it's in today. No matter who or what you think caused your despair, it's you who ultimately made the decision—right or wrong. *What decision?*

We have made collective decisions throughout our lives that got us where we are today. Your choices have all added up together to produce the now.

I'm talking about the many choices we make every day in

a matter of seconds appear to be insignificant, but they have all added up to be the life you now have.

You have made a choice when you didn't pay it; you chewed and swallowed it; you let them tell you what was best for you; you believed it; you prayed for it; you gained the weight; you dropped out; you gave in; you signed it; you hit her; you let him; you missed the warning signs; you accepted it; you didn't make clear what you wanted; you talked yourself into believing it; you went; you raised him; you left her; you picked him; you didn't require enough of yourself; you gave him the money; you let your dreams get dusty; you spent too much; you gave up; you left too soon; you said it; you settled for less; you trusted her; you lived like you didn't deserve better; you opened the door; you let them run over you; you moved there; you let them control you; you wanted the car; you borrowed it; you let her manipulate you again; you called her; you chose those friends; you ignored it; you didn't say no; you let them stand in your way; you took the job; you let them run that guilt trip on you again; you stayed; you enabled him; you took her back; and now it is you who lives with it!

These are the subtle and seemingly harmless actions that mold and shape our circumstances. Make better choices in each moment and you will live a better life.

Choosing Wiser

Good choosing consists of calculating in terms of possible outcomes, and positioning ourselves for success. When anything at all is before you, examine what could become of the situation; then decide if you can live with it; because one day, you just may have to. Make no mistake, choosing wisely out of the gate is the most effective way to avoid undesired consequences. But what if you didn't make the best choice at the beginning and now the damage is done?

Here is where we must be brave enough to ask ourselves the toughest accountability question there is:

What was my contribution to this situation?

This is important because when you learn to get the lessons from your tests, you don't have to repeat the course.

Sometimes, without knowing it, we make ourselves available to heartache by sitting in its way. Review how past choices or not choosing have brought you to this present time in your life. And if you aren't ecstatic with the life you have, be disgusted enough to strengthen your hindsight skills.

This is how you do it. Stop living like you've had no other experiences in life to draw from, and build on what you know. Remember, you are a "professional lifer." You know that with each behavior, thought or response comes a consequence. Start to be more mindful of the consequence itself. Sometimes we choose as though our behaviors will have no consequences, but for every action there is a reaction.

Never Make Choices that Position You Poorly

A woman once sacrificed all of her financial assets and her dream to fund the dream of her lover. The arrangement was supposed to be profitable for both of them, but when the dust cleared, she was left with nothing. He, on the other hand, had gained considerable wealth and prestige.

She blamed him for years for her debt and the despair she encountered as a result of his broken promises. Now desperate, she wrote me requesting tips for getting out of the predicament he "put" her in. The truth of the matter was, she hadn't been a total victim in this case.

He couldn't have *put* her into anything without her consent. This situation is a prime example of how we can position ourselves poorly then go into victim mode when things don't work out. She wants it fixed now, but that isn't possible until she takes personal responsibility for how it got broken to begin with. The midst of a meltdown is not the time to blame others, but rather the time to peel back the mishap piece by piece in order to get down to how you participated in the creation of the problem. This can be a very difficult thing to do, and it requires a great deal of courage, but it's necessary. Courage sometimes means swallowing our pride and asking ourselves some uncomfortable questions.

For this woman, it's necessary to ask herself why she thought parting with her dream for someone else's was an appropriate choice to begin with. What was her motivation to risk it all? What was it about her thinking that she failed to explore even the slightest possibility of losing everything should the investment go sour? Where was her head? Where was her heart? And why?

She must search out the deep belief within herself that guided her into this unwanted direction. When we're brave enough to evaluate how we got to the places of discomfort, we grow better at living life. Behind every predicament, ask yourself:

What was my thinking here and what about that thinking must I change in order to set myself up for a better next time?

Bad Choices: A Widespread Condition of Defeat

Once, I was speaking to a group of nonviolent offenders. One young man said,"...but how can you be successful when the cops take you down for no reason!" He continued,"One night a bunch of us was just hangin' out on the corner; we was minding our own bitness when the police rolled up and checked one of my boyz. He was carrying a piece [gun]; I didn't even know. I hadn't done nothin' and I didn't have nothin' either. And I told the cops, but they didn't believe me. So they took all of us in! All dis motivation and whatever is okay, but you can't do good when the system won't let you."

I explained to the young man that although he had not committed an actual crime, he was in fact guilty.

He was guilty of not considering the consequences ahead of time; he was guilty of associating with what seemed unseemly; he was guilty of lingering about aimlessly in the dark with no destination; he was guilty of bouncing lopsided with a lean as though his feet were swollen, and trying to pass that off as a walk; he was guilty of looking sneaky and shifty; he was guilty of not establishing solid credibility before that night; he was guilty of not creating a clear distinction between him and a common thug; he was guilty of being blameworthy; he was guilty of underestimating the power of impression; he was guilty of answering to a nickname related to death; he was guilty of not knowing that others measure the true character of a man by looking at his friends; he was guilty of not having any friends because real ones wouldn't have jeopardized his freedom; he was guilty of knowing someone who would carry an illegal weapon; he was guilty of not knowing anyone honorable enough to vouch for his trustworthiness; and he was guilty of being so cool that he had no room for wisdom. Basically, he was guilty of having no identification of purpose for his life, and that made him guilty by default.

He said, "But that's not fair; I shouldn't be judged by what I look like!" He was now guilty of having a false assumption of what's fair. He was right, and that was the problem. He lived from a creed of what *should* be, in this life, instead of living from what really *is*. It's not fair. Who said it would be? Now what? We often fall into the trap of trying to get others to live according to a set of rules or standards that we think are out there; and maybe in principle we are right, but what have you gained if being right hasn't met up with being happy?

In the Real World Others Judge You by Perception

In our society, a woman might want to think twice about wearing a red leather mini, a tank top, fish net hosiery and six-inch heels to a job interview for teaching elementary school children. Theoretically, this attire doesn't impair her teaching skills and qualifications one way or another; she is as smart as she is, regardless of what she has on. She *should* be able to wear what she wants, but the operative word here is "should." What *should* be in theory is not always what we live in truth. By the way, Erin Brockovich harnesses her own unique talents that transcend average standards. Typically speaking, if a prospective teacher goes for the job dressed as creatively as we've mentioned, it's not likely she'll be hired. Is it fair? Does it really matter?

In the big picture, being right only means something when you are gaining more than losing; so pick your fights carefully. What good is winning the battle if you're losing the war? Why would anyone bother challenging insignificant stuff at the expense of overall happiness?

Here, the aspiring school teacher valued teaching. Then dress the part, teach and be fulfilled. The "juvenile offender" wanted his freedom. If picking up his pants, putting on a belt, leaving the house when he actually has somewhere to go with people who are going somewhere keeps him out of patrol cars, why not just do it? In this society, the bottom line is you can't look gangster but cry alter boy.

An Ounce of Prevention Is Worth a Pound of Cure

We know that you simply can't repair the problems in your life until you have repaired the mindset that created them. Consider our broken-hearted woman who gave up her dreams for her lover. She wants to "fix" her life now. By "fixing," we mean replenishing and restoring her life *back* to the way it was. Perhaps she wants her money returned and an explanation for why he lied, or maybe she even wants him back!

Like most people, she has a mentality to fix her mess only after the fact. People don't often realize that "fixing" does nothing to prevent the same type of situation from happening again...

...And it cost you, time, money and quality of life!

"Fixing" is merely patch-working *beneath* your actual breakthrough. "Fixing" is busy work, and there is no real gain in that. When we concentrate our efforts on *fixing* the aftermath rather than preventing its creation, we stay stuck.

You can't use a short-term solution for a repetitive problem. Whatever emotional issues the woman had that enabled her to choose poorly to begin with will come back again and again, somewhere in her life, if they aren't addressed at the root. When you don't change how you think, you won't change how you feel, and you will continue to experience lack somewhere on some level—in your relationships, your finances and your work.

This brings us to another defeating aspect of *fixing*. It puts you "back on track." This means to get back whatever you think you lost. But trying to get "back on track" depletes energy, leaving nothing left over to get ahead. Besides, we aren't trying to get back on track; that means to go back where we came from, and we don't want that anymore. We want to move beyond where we were. So stop weeding your garden. Stop finding temporary solutions to patch up long-term problems. It's a waste of your time. Instead, use your efforts to develop a system that will keep your garden free of weeds.

So if you want to change your life, change your incentives, your purposes and your accountability. To change the outcomes of your external world, you must reengineer the internal structure that produced it. Then you will be well on your way to the life you deserve.

De-excusilize Yourself

"De-excusilize"(dee-excuse-zah-lize) is a word I coined that means to stop making excuses for why things don't work. It means to free yourself of excuses much like you would clear rubbish from a machine. To de-excusilize is to give up justifying and blaming. It means that you now are committed to finding reasons why you can make it happen and why you can deliver, as opposed to having excuses for why you can't.

Practice de-excusilizing. It's this quality that makes ordinary people extraordinary. People who have pledged themselves to excellence find ways to be productive no matter what. Anybody can fall feeble to obvious limitations, but how crafty and clever can you be at making things work when it looks like there's no way?

Did you know that a young James Earl Jones had a speech impediment? Back then, it's possible that people excused him from success, believing he couldn't do well for himself. People will excuse us if we allow it. They offer pity and expect nothing from you when you have visible challenges, but James Earl Jones didn't wallow in the pity and vindicate himself. He found ways to develop his voice; in fact, he's famous for having an inflection and deep resonance that we associate with royalty. And because of this, he often plays the role of a king in hollywood as he did for Mufasa in *The Lion King*, as well as the King of Zimunda in Eddie Murphy's *Coming to America*.

Avoid buying into the excuse-making that others assign to us. You don't want to be let off the hook. Expect the best from yourself and let people see that you're committed to your welfare. Never allow anyone to put you on the side lines. You don't want or need a release from greatness.

Most People Don't Expect the Best from Themselves

Instead, they treat explanations as though they're as good as victory itself. They emphasize what they can't do, and they give you a list of obstacles that explain why life doesn't work. Please acknowledge that announcing your problem doesn't replace the need to solve it. Good excuses don't stand in the gap for real success. Life rewards action only.

Far too often, we overly entertain the struggle. We must be mindful not to become enamored with your own neurosis. It's fine to be sensitive to the complications of your past, but not to the extent of hindering your future. The deep blue sea of sorrow can be dangerously fascinating, but it's now time to swim to shore. You can't afford to be crippled by your own infirmities. Instead, overcome them.

Yours is to amaze beyond perceived limitations. The only way to do that is to believe there is a way and commit to finding it. Besides, we get no credit for the drama no matter how legitimate it is. Some of the experiences I had as a child were unfortunate, but still none of it entitled me to be let off the hook.

As children, our lives are produced and directed by someone else. As adults, we must move ourselves forward. For me, growing up and becoming a woman meant I could have a brand new slate. I was the new producer doing a different film now. Once in charge, I could and would expand the budget, change the script, lights, cameras, wardrobe, cast members and location. Now that the chair had my name on the back, I made a conscious choice to create, with my life, a blockbuster hit! And so it is with you.

You are blameless for your childhood experiences, and you shouldn't have to spend some of your adulthood patching the holes in your life that someone else created simply because they hadn't healed from their own emotional deficiencies. There is no justice for coping with pain today that was inflicted on you when you were vulnerable and new to this world. But please know this: If you really want a healthy, wealthy and meaningful life, you have to look to no one for restitution.

Don't Expect to Be Compensated for the Harm

Don't waste your life holding your mouth open and your hands out. Doing so prolongs agony. You must take on the task of healing and fixing your life, even those things you didn't break. Because if anything is stopping you, you alone are losing. You have to own the responsibility of making the rough places plain for yourself. Do this for you. The short of it is, things happened, and by the grace of God it's now over. The good news is the past is gone, and it never has to be your future! Besides, no matter what you have gone through, who has wronged you and what appears to be a loss, you get no recognition for your challenges unless you conquer them.

Honestly, would you be reading this book if it were

entitled, *How I Struggled at 26—A step-by-step guide for acquiring worry, debt and loneliness at any age?* Probably not. You are reading to hear what it took to rise above the obstacles and live prosperously, but I wouldn't be able to share anything insightful had I elected to be a victim of life.

Please keep this in mind during your day to day living. Nobody wants to be grilled and bombarded with the tall tales of how life is hard. If you want merits for your suffering and medals of honor for your affliction, find ways to heal.

Plant Your Seeds No Matter What!

Be the hero or shero in your life and not the one with the best explanations for why things didn't workout for you. Besides, concentrating on tribulation gets you more of the same. Focusing on what doesn't work permeates the situation and invites lack into your life all the more! This is the way our minds operate. Whatever you think about, you will draw to yourself. Concentrate on what you have rather than what you don't have. Move away from contemplating what's lacking from your life and identify what isn't. And you will draw affluence.

Maybe this book finds its way to you during a time when things are going well or maybe you are truly in the eye of the storm. Wherever you are, know that you have to fit your dreams in your schedule anyhow. It is a universal principle that everything operates on an input-output method. In other words, "You reap what you sow." I'm not making reference to the vengeance we usually mean when referring to this adage. Here, I'm talking about the basic principle of producing. It's a fundamental law of nature, agriculturally speaking, that if you don't sow a seed, you don't reap a crop. Even when you have the most understandable reason for not producing, the results are the same. No seed, no crop.

You have to make a way, find a way, create a way, design a way. Discover an avenue to start and run your business, find a way to go back to school, find a way to advance in your career, find a way to strengthen your relationships regardless of challenges. Because again...no seed, no crop. The seed of success must get in the ground and be cultivated in order to grow. You have to work your fields, between, through and around all the drama, or you will not have a harvest time.

Any farmer will affirm this truth. Regardless of the level of tragedy, the legitimacy of the event or nature of the excuse, if nothing gets planted, nothing will grow. I'm not suggesting that challenges can't get to you. I know better. I'm saying don't let them get the *best* of you. Live larger than your hardships by instantly rebounding from them. Waste no time stewing, pitying, or being shaken up. Instead, brush yourself off and get back into the game inside of the very moment you fell to the ground!

You Don't Have to Be an Extraordinary Person
Just Do the Extraordinary Thing!

The extraordinary thing is to work your dreams during the most inconvenient times of life. When your circumstances get hard, and your faced with opposition, do two things. First, ask yourself, *"What would the average person do in this situation?"* Then second, avoid that, and do what an extraordinary person would do.

If the average person needs thirty minutes to prepare, you need fifteen; if the average person is going to be on time, then you'll be early, if the average person is going to do it tomorrow, you'll do it today. If the average person doesn't finish what they start, you will finish ahead of time. While the average person is complaining, immerse yourself in problem solving. While the average person is not following up, you're following through. With practice, it becomes easier to determine what the average person will do. To help get better attuned to how people respond to life, here are some generic profiles:

Sixty percent of Americans (the average person) believe that they are thinkers, wish to win, can't take criticism, hate change and they live for the weekend. They typically have no deliberate plan of action. Instead, they continuously struggle while hoping things will work out for the best. They just pray that nothing bad happens to them as they wait for their ships to come in. While waiting on their miracle, they live on auto-pilot, play it safe and risk nothing. "One day things will get better," they say. Some profess to be "waiting on the Lord." The only problem is, they fill their lives with so many excuses they fail to notice when He comes!

Then there are the twenty-seven percent group. They would rather die than think. They never win and their only goal in life is to make sure no one else does. They tend to be very cynical, negative, defensive, inconsiderate, critical and incapable of admitting mistakes. They are usually irresponsible, suspicious of other peoples' motives, terrible listeners, argumentative, combative, and poor team members. Needless to say, we don't want to practice any of these unsuccessful habits. So then, to whom can we look to be inspired?

Ten percent of this country are our thinkers. They enjoy problem solving. They sometimes win because they plan well. They know how to consider and study their strategies before doing the work. Not being fans of risk taking, they tend to win with a great deal of effort. Although it takes them a long time to do it, many of them know how to gradually create wealth. They are the good old-fashion savers who still have their first buck!

Then there are the remaining three percenters. These are people who have worked on themselves and have risen from twenty-seven, sixty and ten percent groups in order to be well groomed trail-blazing victors. When an achiever's ship doesn't come in, she swims out to it. They don't take "no" for an answer; they take it for a vitamin! They are doers who plan to, expect to and always do win.

They constantly seek to improve themselves and, because of this trait, they make a lot of mistakes. But being optimistic allows them to turn their errors into triumph. They have tremendous energy and are exceptionally happy about life. They have a positive self-image and are excellent communicators. These goal-oriented, persuasive leaders are capable of admitting when they've made a mistake. They tend to be generous with giving approval and compliments to others; they learn from their experiences, have high levels of confidence, are self-motivators, honest with themselves about their own weaknesses and aren't sensitive to criticism.

The average person cringes at the thought of hearing criticism, but it can be quite valuable if you stay focused on the big picture. I believe you are a person who seeks improvement; you simply wouldn't read a book like this unless you were committed to personal development. Since growth is your mission, make things a little easier on yourself by letting others help.

Shakespeare says, "The eye can't see itself." Often, others can see weaknesses that we're just too close to identify. A few minor adjustments might be the very thing you need to elevate your life.

You can be empowered by all of this information and discover ways to make your dreams happen. Unlike the victim, become adept at finding solutions when they aren't necessarily obvious. After a while, you will enjoy working out challenges. It will be much like child's play—a game or puzzle you've mastered, and you know how to win. The good news is, there is always a way. But we must be willing to de-excusilize and find it!

CHAPTER 7

Escaping the Hidden Traps that Can Make and Keep You Broke

We know that self worth and taking personal responsibility for our lives is necessary. But be aware of the "loose end" traps that can creep into your life while you're working on yourself.

Trap #1: Can't Say "No"

The most common trap that stops many from excelling is the inability to say no. Have you ever said "okay" when you really wanted to say no? Why didn't we just say no? I submit, it's because you want others to like you, depend on you, see you as capable and dependable. Sometimes you find the courage to actually say no, but then spend so much time feeling guilty about it that you may as well had said yes. This seems like a simple and harmless issue but the "disease to please" can be immobilizing.

I know a woman in her early eighties who spent her entire

life pleasing other people at her own expense. She never once fulfilled her dreams because of the obsessive need to be accommodating. Without saying a word, she married who her mother chose, even though she wanted someone else; without saying a word, she lived in a house her husband picked, even though she desired something else. Never feeling entitled to make a decision went on and on for years. She thought having an opinion would cause people to dislike her. For her, speaking her mind meant being confrontational and difficult. So to avoid rejection, her method of operation was to be agreeable and yielding even as it went against her better judgment.

It's a major hindrance when we fear rejection to the extent of bartering away our lives. It is then that we become everything to everybody to the point of exhaustion. We even sing along with Chaka and Whitney, "I'm every woman it's all in me, anything you want done baby, I do it naturally..." We go on, "...I can read your thoughts right now—from A to Z." Now, I like that song, but it's only a song. I think in many aspects we've accepted it as a standard of living. Go ahead and enjoy the song, but keep it in perspective. We have to be careful not to develop a "god complex." That is to say, that you do it all.

You read minds, build skating rinks, settle storms, save dolphins, solve crimes, bathe helicopters, braid pasta, and in your spare time, serve as everyone's medicine cabinet, professional leader, relationship expert, and financial counselor! This is a widespread concern because most people desperately need the approval and acceptance of others. This all stems back to the issues of unworthiness we discussed before. Nobody wants to be rejected; so here again we see the need to be grounded in self-worth.

Rejection doesn't Mean that You are Unwanted

I maintain that rejection does not exist in that context. I believe rejection is the natural filtering process that weeds people out of your life who can't support you loving yourself. So, it's not personal. Rejection isn't necessarily bad news. Consider a body that needs a kidney transplant. All empirical data suggests the operation will be successful. However, after the surgery, the doctors find that the body *rejected* the kidney. Was the body bad? Was the kidney bad? No; the two were just incompatible. And so it is in life. When your priorities clash with those of other people's, it's not bad. You're just different and incompatible. And in this time and space the relationship is not a match.

You have to get around to saying no. When you don't say no to anybody for anything ever, you find yourself postponing your own dreams. We make excuses about how busy we are, but how is anyone ever too busy to be first in their own life? What in the world could be more important than spending time becoming your highest self?

We must be committed to ourselves as a first priority. When people ask for favors, time, money or anything else that requires you extend yourself, consider what it will cost you emotionally. Otherwise, you cheat yourself out of valuable living. What personal dreams or goals are you delaying while you're making-nice and trying to be liked? Know that placing boundaries are essential when you want to be successful. So if you are over extending at your own expense, examine why.

Do you feel that other people's opinions, thoughts and needs are more valuable than yours? If so, it's necessary to incline your self worth in order to realize the value of your own time and plans. When you start to *feel* rather than just *say* it's your perfect right to pursue your own interests, it becomes much easier to say no to others. Also, we should be able to make choices for our lives—guilt free.

When saying no brings about feelings of guilt it's important to explore these feelings. After all, for what reasons would guilt be present? What could you have possibly done that relinquishes your privilege to live fulfilled? Are you not entitled to experience happiness and make the best of your own existence?

For many years it's been believed that saying *no* means you're restrictive, non-supportive, mean or uncooperative. This isn't true. When you practice saying no, you begin to feel the benefits of having some of your life back. How can this be wrong? Often times saying no up front prevents us from disappointing others on the back end. When you tell people yes all the time, then for one reason or another you can't or don't come through, you develop a habit of letting folks down. In which case, everyone is disappointed, including you because it's probably not your intention to be unreliable. So then, it's always best to say no in the beginning if initially you have reservations. Do only what you really want to do in life, and let the rest go.

If you're not taking the time to get whole because you're trying to be a good friend, remember real friends want you to do what is necessary for you to be your best. And they won't require anything of you that's contrary to that. Also, don't worry about being obligated. Let friends bring what they can to the relationship as you bring what you can. When the love is real and mutual, your best will be good enough. In essence, there is no place for pressure or manipulation in a healthy friendship. Real friends don't give ultimatums or make demands. Bottom line, real friends don't keep score.

What does this have to do with being Broke?

You simply bring more to the table of any relationship as well as any endeavor, financially or otherwise, when you're in your best shape emotionally, physically, spiritually, and psychologically. It's just not possible to reach optimal levels of fulfillment if you're drained from being overused. So, practice saying no.

How you do this is by being and staying true to your first reaction to a request. You don't have to answer immediately. Take the time you need to decide what's comfortable for you. If you don't feel you're being given an opportunity to make a decision, that is a sign in and of itself.

Choose how You will Share Yourself

You should be able to make decisions about your time without feeling rushed or bullied. It's your responsibility to know when your plate is full, and it's up to you not to allow someone's procrastination to become your personal emergency. So you are entitled time to think about what's being asked of you. If they can't wait, don't hold them up; let them move on to the next person. It isn't necessary to justify nor have others approve of your choices. You don't need a scholarly explanation for needing time to think things over or for giving a no answer. Your decisions are *self* explanatory, and that's enough. If something does not sit well with you, it just doesn't. If you are not comfortable with a matter. You just aren't. Explaining is unnecessary especially when the listener isn't willing to take no for an answer. If you find it easier to say no by justifying yourself first, do what works for you; but remember, "no" is a complete sentence.

The easiest way to say no is to have your own personal agenda to which you can look forward. It's a lot easier to decline the requests of others when you have a burning desire to do your own thing. But you have to know what your own thing is. Make a priority list for what you want out of life. What are your values? What are your goals? And what steps are you going to take in order to achieve them? Working on these things will make the best use of your time. It is here that saying no to others will eventually mean saying yes to yourself!

What are You Losing?

Decide what saying yes to others too frequently has cost you, then make a list of those times and the consequences of each. Remember, saying no does not have to be harsh. We want to be assertive, not aggressive. Say it the way you want to hear it, and you'll reduce the risk of offending people. All it means to be assertive is to adopt a "You are valuable, I am valuable" mindset into your marketplace of understanding. Your needs matter as much as the next person. I agree with Brian Tracy who says: "I am better than no one; but no one is better than me."

Trap #2: Carrying Old Baggage

The most effective way to avoid falling into this trap and having it consume you, is to forgive.

I know this first hand. This trap had been my chief personal challenge. Old baggage is the accumulation of unfulfilled expectations and broken promises that others made to us or we made to ourselves. We hear a lot about forgiveness and how it's to our benefit to do so, but that's easier said than done. Once feelings of frustration and disappointment are embedded into our hearts, it's difficult to *un*invite them. It can be hard to just "let go"of pain caused by feeling used, lied to, lied on, talked about, humiliated, unprotected, cheated or deceived.

People Hold Grudges because there's a Pay Off

It can feel like sweet revenge when you stay angry with someone who has wronged you. Sometimes, we think of it as punishment when we deny them our affections, conversation or presence. But the truth is, to hold on to animosity is like "You taking poison and hoping they will die." I used to beat down on myself for not being able to stay mad at people after they had offended me. I used to feel like a submissive jellyfish when I found myself laughing and talking with them again. But after some growth, I realized it's a good thing when you can instinctively release bitterness. It's not a sign of weakness but an illustration of strength to have reflex compassion.

It takes courage to forgive, but your strength comes in knowing that it's possible and it's necessary. Holding on to past experiences gone sour, retards your financial and physical growth.

Some metaphysicians believe that a lack of forgiveness is the reason for many illnesses—specifically, arthritis.

What does this have to do with being broke? If we don't feel well, it stands to reason that we will not see financial opportunities. It's just difficult to make money, or be fulfilled when you're in pain. Therefore, to avoid this trap, it's required that you complete relationships and obtain closure for yourself once and for all.

People ask me sometimes, "How did you learn to forgive behind your experiences?" The truth is, initially I didn't know I needed to. Remember, for the bulk of my life, I'd subconsciously numbed out, put myself on automatic pilot and achieved some goals despite it all. I had no clue I had been neglected. I experienced deprivation for so long that I stopped feeling. I was in such denial that I didn't even know I was lying. I felt alone; but I didn't know it. I was disappointed in everybody; but I didn't know it. I had baggage; but I didn't know it. I had created a false-self that kept me from recognizing pain; but I didn't know it.

I had no connection with my own feelings. Emotion and I were strangers who had never met because I didn't have time; I was too busy surviving. It was this detachment, along with being an ambitious, resourceful, enterpriser that kept me above water through the years, and on the surface I had been handling things well.

Eventually, I realized that I wasn't reaching a genuine place of happiness. Something had to change. What I knew for sure was that staying above water just wasn't good enough anymore. Merely surviving doesn't make a life. It was time for my true Self to come forth. Endurance had gotten me as far as it could, and I was grateful. But now, it was time to feel. Without feeling, I couldn't forgive, and I would never have gotten on the path of becoming the total woman I was meant to be. So in short, you have to be sick and tired of what isn't working enough to do something different. Holding on to the past just isn't worth it when you consider what's at stake. At some point you have to accept people where they are.

People are Exactly Who they Are

It's unreasonable to expect people to be or do anything except what they have shown you they'll be and do. This applies to everyone.

Consider my parents. They were my parents sure enough, but gods they were not. They weren't perfect beings incapable of making poor choices. My mother was just a woman who, whether she was aware of it or not, believed she was ugly, inferior, weak, and unworthy of staying alive. My mother didn't love herself. And a mother who undervalues her own existence can't teach her child any thing different.

Daddy was just a man who had his own self-esteem deficiencies. Why else would a bright and talented individual prey on insecure women?

Daddy couldn't be still either. For him, disappearing distracted others from seeing what he believed were his shortcomings. Running also kept him creating the illusion of getting things done when, in all actuality, he wasn't. He couldn't see how to create a life of splendor for himself using his gifts, or maybe he wasn't confident that he even had gifts. In his own words, he had "nothing to give." The more he said that, the more it became true. Daddy told people this up front with both his words and his actions. Few of us listened. Instead, we continued to expect him to be different. We expected him to be responsible. That just wasn't who my father was. Both Momma and Daddy did their best being who they were. What more could anyone expect?

People's actions come from their true beliefs, and beliefs are the source of what determines us. If they had believed differently about themselves, they would have reacted and

161

responded differently to their needs, my needs and the world in general. How could I blame them for not having the ability to think outside of themselves. *The Richest Man in Babylon* by George Clason says, "Our acts can be no wiser than our thoughts, and our thinking can be no wiser than our understanding."

After these considerations, I'd met the power of forgiveness. And I began feeling compassion for all who had "wronged" me. These people had done the best they could with their own baggage and infirmities; and yes, their best was less than what I needed at the time. But now I know it wasn't personal, and that made all the difference in the world.

Also answering this question for myself helped me to forgive: *What did they do right?* Everyone comes into your life to teach you something. Rather than viewing their presence in my life as a disadvantage, I found it better to concentrate on what I learned about myself as a result of knowing them. It can be difficult to do this part. We know the negative stuff like a favorite song, but can you itemize what they did to enhance your life? What do you now know, have, or feel as a result of this person, these people, this thing happening to you?

Girdled with a new empathy and tenderness for my parents, and with knowing they did their personal best, I was able to shift my concentration from what they did wrong, bad, and cruel, over to what they did that ultimately served me. I was angriest with my mother, so I started forgiving her first by making a list of the goods things that came with her mothering.

I think she demonstrated love when she stood on her swollen legs with ulcers and dug through the Flinstone vitamin bottle, looking for my favorite character. I think she loved me when she helped with my speeches. It was love

Join Asha's VIP Club FREE at **www.ashatyson.com** *for further support*

when she served as PTA (Parent Teacher Association) president when I was in fifth grade. Her leadership skills were matchless, and when she boldly called her meetings to order, I felt like the daughter of a national celebrity. Love is what had her find me a classy summer camp to attend, instead of one that was short of funds, unorganized and ran like a low priority project for poor kids.

She showed me love every Easter Eve when she took the time to boil and decorate eggs. An Easter egg hunt would be certain to take place the next morning, even though pain had shot through her feeble body all night long. Love was in the curls she meticulously formed in my hair each time I was to stand before an audience. And whether or not she did so intentionally, I think it was because she loved me that she stayed alive until I was self-sufficient, safe and secure.

None of the telephone rings that had made me jump for more than twenty-five years was ever "the call." No one had to inform me that my mother was gone. She had held on and waited until I could be there myself. I knew Momma was expiring when the intensive care visiting hours didn't apply to me anymore. Even when I arrived at 4:00 a.m., instead of the medical staff asking me out, they compassionately provided pillows, blankets, apple juice and jazz music. After six nights of watching momma lose her battle with Sickle Cell Anemia, she peacefully made her transition one winter morning as I held her hand and thanked her for just…being. Her exit was unintrusive, dignified and graceful. She didn't leave a lonely little girl afraid in the world. And I loved her for that. I loved her.

My mother wasn't a monster, and sure as all of us, she made mistakes; but I could forgive. She was what God had given me, and I would take her all over again to be who I am today.

I continued the forgiveness process for Daddy, then other relatives and so on. The more I let go, the easier it got.

Be Encouraged

Although it may be difficult initially, you do harness the power to forgive, but it's up to you to use it. It will take as long as you decide it needs to. Depending on your sense of urgency to get on with your life, you can change you mind about how you feel in this very second! Go ahead and forgive them. Forgive all of them, and use that energy to create the life of your dreams. Forgive anyone, dead or alive who you may be resenting. Forgive your parents, caregivers, siblings, aunts, uncles, spouses, cousins, your husband, your wife, your significant or insignificant others, your ex's, teachers, the fraternity, the sorority, landlords—past and present, bankers, counselors, co-workers, former and current bosses, neighbors, church members, community leaders, friends, enemies, everyone, anyone! Just make an agreement with yourself to be free!

Remember, the key is to first examine the expectations you had. Then analyze why they didn't meet them. Be careful here. Really think about whether or not they were emotionally, psychologically, physically or even mentally capable of living up to the standards you assigned. Keep in mind, people aren't obligated to live, choose, act or think the way you have prescribed for them. If you didn't have a Donna Reed for a mother, it didn't mean that the one you had was "bad." She was who she was, and Donna was in your head. Our thoughts don't belong to other people, and we don't have to live according to theirs. No one can dictate your behavior but you! And that is the good news, but it works both ways. If you have the ability to set your own standards and choose for your life, so does everyone else. Don't expect others to embrace your passions, philosophies and convictions. They are entitled to have their own.

Next, analyze closely what they did well. How did they contribute to your life? How are you better, stronger, or wiser since knowing them? Discover the mystery inside of what they came to teach you rather than dismissing them as one big inconvenience. As we've discussed, people do the best they can with what they are equipped with. If you see something more they could have or should have done, regardless to how simple or common sense oriented it seemed to you, you didn't see it through their eyes.

The truth is, nobody wants to fall short. We all want to be thought of as talented, smart, attractive, dependable etcetera. People do what they can do, and when their best isn't good enough for us, we somehow think they could have done better. This is where the feelings of unfulfilled expectations creep in. There was no such "better" to be done. No one held out on you. They had not saved the good carpet while giving you remnants; although sometimes it feels like it. Even if they instinctively knew to do better, they may not have had the courage to follow through. Some people *know* but can't seem to bring themselves to do.

Consider the many who struggle with trying to eat "right" and exercise as a part of their lifestyle. But never seem to get around to *doing* it, although they know better. I'm saying, people show up at the battlefield with their biggest guns, prepared to give it their best shot, and they really do *their* best. It's impractical to expect they would meet the standards of *your* best.

Avoid Accumulating New Baggage

In the future, to avoid stock piling new junk, learn to accept people for both who they are and who they're not. You can't fully love anyone when you hold them hostage to your expectations. Make sure you are caring for a person for who they are right now, in this very moment. Otherwise, it isn't them, but who you hope they'll become someday that has you involved. That is not unconditional love. That's love riding on a potential pass.

We know from the discussion of this trap, that it's possible to create a future from a space of nothingness as though you have a fresh, clean life with no historical baggage. And yes, it can be that simple. Just make up your mind that its worth it to rid yourself of what doesn't work for you anymore. Find a bigger pay off in forgiving than you do holding on to the past. After all, what do you have to lose, except baggage?

Trap #3: Regret

Do you ever find yourself entertaining the thoughts of what could have and should have been? Please know that being stuck inside of regret can cost you financially. If you're preoccupied with what you didn't accomplish, you won't have much energy to entertain what can be accomplished. This can make and keep anybody broke!

I recognize that everyone is not in their twenties and that it may feel too late to be talking about living any kind of dream. But please know if you are still here, what you were purposed for is still undone. Your compensation for doing the work is still untapped. Some people think if they had gone to school, waited to have children or had better opportunities and freedoms, life would be grand. They feel that they have had "set backs" in life. But I challenge this notion. There is no such thing as a set back!

A set back presupposes you would have been ahead of where you are now if things had happened differently, but please know that your journey has molded you for your greater good, and it was exactly what it needed to be. There was no set back, and there is no failure if you learned anything at all from the experience. The road you took was the one you needed in order to get where you belong. But Asha,"...if only I had known what I know now..." I get where you are coming from if you feel this way, and at the offset, it sounds sensible. But the truth is, you couldn't have known what you know now without having life happen exactly the way it did for you. What you know now came via this journey, and another one wouldn't have done the trick.

Some people are in a hurry to make up for what they believe to be lost time. And so they have saturated their lives with anxiety and panic. But the good news is, there is no lost time! Everything you are, felt, seen, heard, or been through has all served to shape you into the person you were meant to be. And everything is as it should be.

Consider this: You are driving to visit a friend. Along your path you find that because of the way the streets are designed, you will actually need to pass by your friend's house, swoop around the median in the middle of the road and go back in order to get to her home. You notice this is the only thing you can do because there is no access road that allows you to turn any sooner without passing her house first. Isn't it amazing how we don't think of such deviations as being"out of our way?" We've grown accustom to this being what it means to have a typical driving experience. We don't even classify it as a full fledge detour when it's an issue of a median, a"one-way" street or a "no left turn" that prohibits us from going directly to our destination. We understand that these are simply the rules of the road and it's necessary to comply with them to get where we're going. So, the route you took was not a set back but a required action in order to reach your goal. And it's not something that took you out of your way; it was just the way you had to go to get where you were going. And so it is with your life.

You must factor in the challenges you face along your journey. Your experiences are not setbacks, but are in fact the way you had to go to get where you were going. And there was no arriving without them. There is no short-cutting to life. It took each and every situation you have encountered to bring you to the now. And now is right on time. There are no set backs—only set ups! You are set up to make the next step toward your purpose. So relax and enjoy the journey. When you move too fast, you miss the lessons. When the lessons are missed, you don't get to graduate to the next phase of your life until you get what was meant for you at the last one. The sooner you tune in and learn whatever you were intended to, the sooner you get to move on in the school of life. As you grow, you get better at the lessons and enjoy life more and more. I have learned to see challenges as a series of lessons; I believe these inquisitions that meet up with us every day are the way life is suppose to be. And they come to enhance not to destroy us. With this, I know I will always be okay.

Another key point when considering regret is to be mindful not to compare yourself to others. Resist that destructive pastime like the plague. Comparing contaminates your self-esteem and is never worth the time it takes. You don't need that. Understand that everyone is in a different place, and what's a breeze for you may be a definite challenge for me. But because we are all free spontaneous choosers, we're all equal. Each and every one of us has the divine privilege to exercise our own free will at any given time. This is the most sacred benefit of being human. You can change your mind in any moment you wish! In every second of your life you have the power to make things better for you!

So run your own race using the portion of perseverance necessary to transcend your unique blend of circumstances. Never worry about what others have or don't have that seems to make it easier for them. Your focus is to muster up the courage to beat your own odds. You can do this if you always keep in the forefront of your mind: No matter what the challenge before me, I will acknowledge each and every one as being another rung in my ladder and not a road block in my way. Concentrate on the resources you have to work with, and not the ones you don't.

Please be mindful that comparing yourself to others also ignites jealously. It's essential that if and when you look at another person's life, you do so with the intention of reminding yourself what's possible for yours. Be grateful for how the "well doers" have lived their lives as it can represent hope for you. Get excited about what their success means. What it means is that success is available; it's possible. It was possible for somebody in this world. And if it's possible for anybody at all, it's also possible for you! And because of the well doer, you now have proof!

It took me a long time to understand the concept of envy. It hadn't been one of my personal challenges. I always believed I was capable of doing anything I saw anybody else do. Seeing prosperity, happiness, fulfillment, love and joy in another person's life reminded me that God hadn't run out of blessings. I didn't see any benefit to jealousy, so I had no use for it in my life. But I didn't know this was not the general perspective of everyone else. Surprisingly, I learned that some people see other's successes as a threat and are therefore jealous of them. But know that jealously, like a disease, can eat away at vitality and cause creative energy to become obstructed. Also, negativity that's channeled towards a person who's being envied, is always returned to the sender. So, please be careful.

We know that regretting is not profitable, but neither is it practical. The "Things would be better if only" theory has zero consistency. There is no guarantee being privy to any of life's "perks" would have sculpted a better you. We can all think of far too many stories of people who were products of "underprivileged" situations but have come out of them victorious and whole. So learn to welcome your obstacles and become good at finding the jewel of each circumstance instead of the inconvenience of it. Doing this will enable you to make a habit of living fuller. I am saying, fastened with self assurance, uncompromised determination and no regrets, you can pick up your buckets right where you are and move forward successfully using whatcha got!

CHAPTER 8

How and Where to Find Your Wealth

Some people and I were out having dinner; we began discussing the creation of this world and our places in it. I shared my thoughts: I believe vitality on earth is a brilliant concept. And I'm positively overjoyed that Somebody thought it would be beneficial to include little ole' me! What a honor. Of all the marvelous creations, I too was allowed to join in!

Someone greater than me thought I could make a contribution here. Even though for years I was clueless as to what that was suppose to be, I wasn't going to be arrogant enough to second guess my existence. Mine was to get busy looking for why I'd been expressed as a living soul. As Robert Browning tells us, "We are not to remake ourselves but to make the absolute best of what God already made."

Another person at the table disagreed. She said, not only was the making of this world a bad idea, but it was even worse that she was here. There was a stillness behind her statement. Sorrow had filled the entire space. And I couldn't think of one single solitary thing to say. We all felt compassion for her. I was compelled to try and understand what conjured the depth of her pain.

People Are Not Satisfied

I find that people aren't usually thrilled with the lives they're leading. They are irritable and disappointed. Much of this is because somewhere deep within each of us, we know there's something more we could be doing with our lives. But what? And where do you find the time to ponder the meaning and purpose of your life when you're constantly having to worry about making ends meet?

Frustration builds when you don't feel there's time to follow your destiny. After awhile, you're not sure if you even see it anymore. The only question in your mind when bills are due, the car needs repair, you want to buy your own home or the one you have has a mortgage is...*Where can I get some money?* This chapter will answer that. The answer to where to find wealth is quite simple really.

Where you find wealth is inside of your passion for life. The secret is in knowing the right question to ask. Yours is not to ask, *What can I do to make money?* but rather, *How can I best serve in my purpose?* Finding where you're to give of yourself in the world is the key. Great abundance comes from the energy of your desire to edify, mend and heal.

What I'm suggesting is that you consider shifting your focus from trying to get paid, to trying to be of service. This is a powerful concept. It's the service we render to others that validates we ever existed at all. Having money besides is just one of the fringe benefits. If getting, having, and keeping money is removed from being the center focus of your thoughts, what would replace it? If money were no object, what would then be the subject of your attention?

Service in this context, doesn't mean you should always give away your goods, talents and services for free, or even at a discount. How and when you do charity work should be a personal choice motivated by your own devotion. It's perfectly acceptable to be compensated for your intelligence. In fact, the laws of prosperity are set up so that you will be. What *service* means, however, is to give of yourself generously without the intention of getting what you can out of the endeavor, but rather to put all you can into it. Becoming wealthy is merely one of the results of the latter. Your intention is what is key here. Ask yourself what your real motives are, and examine whether or not they're primarily self-serving. Sure, we go into a situation knowing we desire to be paid for our labor, but financial gain is not to be the chief focus of your deed.

Now I must ask you, have I been presumptuous with this whole service thing? Do you really want to be of service? After all, you could have your own reasons for not wanting to serve.

Being charitable has become trendy and sporty, I know; but aside from that do you really care to extend yourself? Are there ever times you simply aren't interested in sharing? Sometimes we just don't feel like giving to others, especially if we don't see where anyone has done anything for us. But it's taboo to say that out loud. People don't discuss it for fear that they'll be seen as selfish or callous. So we have three kinds of people. Some who have mastered the true art of giving; some who give because we're told we should; and some who just don't give at all.

Soulwork Means Telling Yourself the Truth

Get honest answers that will enable you to move forward to a real and healthy place in your life. So let's get down to earth with ourselves. Do you ever feel as though you are the one who does all the giving, but no one can or will reciprocate the favors when it's your turn? Have you ever gotten fed up with giving, giving, giving, and now you feel like "everyone for himself; God for us all?" If you have resigned to a "live and let live" disposition because you're tired of being the only contributor, know that you're not alone.

Many people at one time or another have subconsciously cut themselves off from others to keep from being hurt or taken for granted. These feelings can result when anyone...family, people you thought were friends or even folks you didn't know well, repeatedly used you as a shoulder to cry on, lean on, build on, step on or even spit on. Although these feelings are valid if you have them, they can hold you back from wealth.

You can't be prosperous with your generosity chip on lock down. Nor can you easily find your purpose in life when you have even a subtle resistance to sharing your goods with the world. This is why:

When you have shifted your concentration from prosperity over to trying to avoid being someone's fool again, your bitterness will trigger you into a rut. While in this space, we've literally become too busy being watch dogs over our hearts, that we have no energy leftover to spark our dreams. And as valid as your feelings are, when your life's goals are at stake, it doesn't matter who's right and who's wrong; it doesn't matter the level you feel abused; and it doesn't matter whether or not they show remorse for disrespecting your kindness. You'll have to find a way to get over it— that is, if you want to be "total package rich."

Give Yourself a Break

If doing acts of charity for others doesn't easily come to you, don't be hard on yourself. You have nothing to be

174

ashamed of. Consider doing whatever you do for others, and giving whatever you give to others as a **direct** act of worship to God. This will eliminate your fear of being mistreated or used. This concept takes out the "middle man," so to speak. It allows you to set your sights beyond the individual and be accountable to your Master. If you're giving or doing a favor as you would if God himself had asked you, it's of no importance whether or not any person appreciates or recognizes your goodness. Remember, it's the intention that rules.

Your intention here is to please God by giving Him an offering. The person who received was simply a vessel you used to demonstrate your act of love to your Ruler. God then will reward you accordingly. When you really think about it, the individual has nothing to do with it at all. They can't obstruct your blessing one way or another.

As you elevate and heal, your guards will eventually come down, and you'll be fine with it. You'll feel strong, capable and safe beyond measure, and living on the defensive will become useless to you. So give unto the Lord, and you can't go wrong.

In our present condition, we often think wealth comes from landing the "right" job, in the most lucrative industry. We've been taught to learn particular skills or trades without having any regard for our individual talents, passions, or interests. This is a mistake. Regardless of how profitable an occupation seems or has been for someone else, your experiences will be different and may not be what brings you wealth at all. So ask yourself the questions that will help you pinpoint your ideal work. Do you like what you do? Have you even had time to evaluate it? If not, make time. You deserve to know, and you have to know.

Do you love what you do enough to do it for free? Does it feel like a bonus when they pay you for it? No? Then read on.

Be careful not to measure yourself against an ideal standard. Instead, be in touch with your own authenticity. Just be willing to find you. Although it's possible to accumulate material wealth doing what offers the big bucks, you also run the risk of never being fully satisfied with your life. Why not have both fulfillment and wealth by doing what you love?

When you are not doing your ideal work, you simply can't be the best, and that isn't fair to anyone—especially you. This message isn't intended to promote you to leave your job, but to get you thinking about whether or not you are in *your* rightful place, operating inside of *your* most promising space. Doing a work that isn't your divine assignment is bound to leave you discontent and frustrated. And what more could we expect? Surely, we don't anticipate a perfect fit when wearing another person's shoes.

When you're not aligned with *your* own thing, the discomfort you feel is a signal that something is wrong. In this case, pain is good news! How about that! Pain can be good. It's true; we wouldn't know we needed to make things better if we never got a signal that anything was wrong.

Inside your suitable calling you'll be more productive and efficient. Why? Because you're doing your thing...doing what you were cut out for, and this will increase your finances unquestionably.

Discovering wealth requires evaluating the natural advantages you already have. They will be hints as to where you should be serving. Wealth is not *out* there somewhere waiting to be located. Accessing wealth is within your immediate means right now, even as you read this sentence! But looking desperately for prosperity may have caused you to miss out up until now. Have you ever looked for something in the house that was right in your face all the time, but you had been searching so aggressively that you couldn't find it?

Consider this famous Victorian lecture first told by Russell H. Conwell. This literary classic is still one of the most influential motivational stories ever told. It informs us of the life of Ali Hafed, a farmer, who sold his land in order to travel the world throughout looking for diamonds. His mission had become obsessive and had caused him to abandon his family. But he refused to come home until he found fortune. After traveling extensively, he still hadn't found wealth. He ended up alone and depressed. Now broken spirited, Ali Hafed threw himself into a river and ended his life.

Meanwhile, the man who had purchased the farm from Hafed was living grateful for his newly acquired homeland. He took pride in enjoying his family and relished in the small benefits of the harvest his farm produced. While satisfied and content, one day he found something that would change his life forever. While tilling the soil of his own farm he discovered a diamond mine! The farmer had become wealthy beyond his own imagining. The very riches Hafed looked for in all the earth had always been right in his own backyard.

This parable illustrates how we must believe that possibility lies within us. It's inside of ourselves that we have to began exploring; not *out* there somewhere. What do you already have? Take time to give this some thought. What did you show up with in the world? Where is your wellspring of talent? What's in your backyard?

Examine and savor your passions, interests and dreams. Acknowledge your ingrain creative energy; appreciate yourself and delight in the fruits of your own labor! Ask yourself what gifts are lying dormant within you. If you were to do anything at all, without reservation, fear or consequence, what would it be? Soar with your imagination; dare to do something different; and believe the unbelievable.

You too will discover financial success is under your own nose. Actually, your largest gold mine is between your ears!

Spend quality time thinking about how to provide a service or product that will enhance the lives of others. Unmask and nurture your jewels. Identify ways in which you can bring more value than cost to people. Fill a need, and you'll have more money than you can keep track of by yourself! This sounds simple enough, so what stops so many people?

Are You Afraid of Success?

Most people are afraid of their own success. On the surface, fear of failure looks to be the obvious reason people shy away from their magnificence, but I submit that we aren't as afraid of "blowing it" as much as we are afraid of "blowing up!" Many folks believe that they could work hard and make it to the top, only to fall flat on their faces. What then? Wouldn't it have been better to stay close to the ground so that the plunge wouldn't have been as painful? Absolutely not.

As we've discussed, there's no failure. If an endeavor doesn't turn out as expected, it wasn't suppose to. Take the lesson, build from the knowledge and go on to the next thing. Crying over "spilled milk" doesn't build wealth. We have to move forward. But again, fear of failure isn't the problem, the present condition of lack is a result of fearing success. Although commonly mistaken to be the work of Nelson Mandela, it's Marianne Williamson who tells us...

> Our deepest fear is not that we are inadequate.
> Our deepest fear is that we are powerful beyond
> measure. It is our light not our darkness that

most frightens us. We ask ourselves who are we to be brilliant, gorgeous, talented and fabulous? Actually, who are you not to be? You are Children of God. Your playing small doesn't serve the world. There's nothing enlightened about shrinking so that other people won't feel insecure around you. It is not just in some of us: it's in everyone. And as we let our own light shine, we unconsciously give other people permission to do the same. As we are liberated from our own fears, our presence automatically liberates others...

Now I ask, have you been playing small? If so, know that it does show up in some area of your life. Do you ever back out of endeavors for fear that what's being asked of you requires something you don't believe you're capable of? Do you fear making mistakes or looking ridiculous? Do you settle for writing articles instead of a book? Are you a potential mover and shaker who can't seem to budge? Do others have more confidence in you than you do? Do you hold back, make excuses, sit on the sidelines and wear your weenie suit? The answers to these questions will help you determine if you are ordering your life from the kiddie menu.

Living Large Requires Risk-Taking

We can't play in the big leagues while signing up only for minor ones. It takes courage and faith to step into greatness, and it's easiest to do when you understand that's where you belong. And I promise you, it is where you belong. Micro-living hinders us from excelling on many levels; individually, socially and globally.

As individuals, we miss out on personal fulfillment when we *choose* to diminish ourselves. And whether you are conscious of it or not, please know that in each moment of your life a choice is being made. By the way, doing absolutely nothing is as much a choice as anything. Please don't misunderstand. Doing nothing renders very real results.

Imagine a person who doesn't do anything at all about the plaque on their teeth. They don't brush them, they don't do the dentist thing, they don't do anything. They do nothing to them, and they do nothing for them. They just have teeth. Should they continue to do nothing, they won't have them for very long. That's why even on small scales, it's essential to deliberately and actively *choose* your life's direction. Every choice you make or don't make still renders an outcome.

If you take life as it comes, roll with the punches and aim for nothing, you will hit it head on! Don't settle for something less than what you were meant to have.

Work without passion may or may not bring money, but it will bring agony for sure. So take the time to find your thing. Labor at what you love. Among many benefits, it will promote emotional, financial and physical prosperity. You were designed for this work and when you operate inside of your element, most everything else falls in place.

Doing what thrills your soul, makes you whole. Be true to yourself even when others disagree with your choices. People will tell you that to work at a day care center when you have an engineering degree is absurd! According to standard thinking, the most logical thing would be to suppress your natural desires and do what traditionally makes the most money.

Consider the medical student who wants to be a chef. What is she thinking? Why would anyone give up "real" security to cook! It is this kind of warped thinking that can beat you out of your abundance. Ironically, when you do your passion, you can often earn more than doing work that has a reputation of paying well. But even more than missing out on your unique wealth, there are emotional consequences when working out of your calling.

The Power of the Withheld Talent is Far Reaching

If your purpose goes unfulfilled, you encourage others to withhold as well. This burdens our entire society. Deficiency, much like success, is contagious. We've all heard it isn't good to entertain the company of toxic people. Studies have found that doing so influences your life and can retard your advancement. It stands to reason, if others can help slow you, they can also help grow you. You too have this profound affect on people.

Seeing you live your passion and fulfill your own dreams can encourage those around you; your children, your parents, your peers and even your superiors can all take value from watching you. You give them a front row seat to a living example of what's possible. Permission is sometimes all a person needs to ignite hope. On the contrary, making excuses, living minuscule and complaining about life creates the same domino affect, but the results are negative.

When you play victim, it substantiates the helplessness that many people already feel. Hopelessness is like a virus that's carried in the air. It has caused many to be impatient, frustrated, sicker, lonelier, and more afraid than ever before. Just think, you can do your part to combat this by answering your calling.

Please don't underestimate the long arm of your

contributing capacity. If you're reserving your goods, while others are simultaneously withholding theirs from the world, collectively we also hamper global healing! Here is why:

There is no substitute for your gift to the planet. No one else can do what you are here to do. Just the same, there is no replacement for another person's gift. So then, each of us is holding a piece of an enormous puzzle. If you don't come with your piece, the puzzle will never be complete.

Disasters overwhelm us at the rate of what seems to be hourly. You've seen the evening news, and we've all been repulsed by the tragedies and traumas. And when we see these things, many times we pass the buck by saying, "Somebody ought to do something about that." But notice, Somebody did do something about it; Somebody created you. Now, I do recognize that the emotional poverties that cause destruction will always be with us on some level, but don't let that discourage you. We are still obligated to reach for the cure. None of us are exempt from our individual responsibility to be remarkable. The ultimate goal is to know you left this world having done everything possible to fulfill your high-handed duty.

Living up to your greatness can be frightening, I won't deny that. Fear is and has always been a major distraction from everything and anything good. What we know is that fear of our own magnificence is what corners us. Some people fear not ever being important enough, or loved enough, or successful enough when all is said and done.

Beating Fear

Beating fear is difficult because there is a payoff for living beneath our potential. Living small keeps people fantasizing about why they're stuck. They use smoke and mirrors to lie to themselves and others about ways they could be living, giving, loving and feeling if this and that hadn't happened. Although it feels justifiable in the moment, when others are gone, and we stand alone in our quiet hours with ourselves, our souls hang wide open. It is then we must be honest about the lives we are leading, and if you aren't pleased with what you see, no excuse matters. With this, you are to throttle forward overcoming any fear, guilt, or shame with the truth.

The truth is, we all have the apparatus to be more powerful than anything that comes up against us. Wealth is found by unloading all doubt and unlocking your internal creativity. You must strengthen your ingenuity muscle by welcoming your inventive thoughts, even when others might consider them strange or unlikely. Also, be loving with yourself whether you're having an overflow, a trickle or a drought of ideas. It's important to be patient with your mind and respect its delicacy.

Gently Pose the Right Questions to Yourself

Ask your self: "What is my passion?" Since we know nothing is by chance, and no two people are exactly alike—not even "identical" twins, what could your presence on earth be about? The answers to these questions require searching out your deep desires. It is helpful to examine your most subtle behaviors. What tendencies do you automatically exhibit? What parts of life do you naturally gravitate to? What do you dream about? What do you prefer to think about? What do you do with your time when you have a choice in the matter? And by now I hope I've helped to affirm, you always have a choice in the matter.

Take inventory of the activities you enjoy whether you've had time to do them or not. What parts of your work do you currently appreciate (besides the paycheck), and what of it would you discard if possible? What abilities, talents or skills come natural to you while others seem to struggle? Examine the experiences in your life. Which ones did you find particularly pleasurable? What do you most often have an opinion about? What clubs or associations would you join if you found the time? What would you do for free if you could be certain of financial security? Inside these answers are the keys to freedom and wealth, and only you can do this for yourself.

Once you find your unique purpose, no one can beat you at it, with it or to it. The beauty in our gifts is that they're ours exclusively! A person could be in the same profession or industry doing the same kind of work as you, but yours will always have a different spin of expression. Therefore, in this respect, there is no such thing as competition!

There will be people who will want only your stuff. There will be some who will want your services or products along with those of your colleagues. This is all fine. There is more than enough affluence for everyone, and what is for you, you will have! No one can ever take what is rightfully yours. This is what I call "divine match marketing." It means when you were born, you were equipped to do your purpose. Meanwhile, the need for your particular brilliance and the people who would benefit from it, had already been earmarked as yours! To deliver your gift to these people is why you are with us, and no one can reach them the way you can.

Please Don't Deny the World

Give us your song, your shop, your business, your idea, your growth. There is something only you can give and without it, someone is being disallowed a healing, a laugh, an uplift—a better quality of life. Besides, denying your calling and procrastinating against it, is the same as rejecting God in slow motion. But there is a better option.

One of the fundamental privileges of being human is having the freedom of choice, and you can *choose* to live your passion right now! God isn't going to fasten us down and bully us into doing our purpose; he did his job by giving us one. Yours is to find what that is and commit it to excellence.

Struggling Can Be Alleviated

Get connected with your divine work. Living on purpose is synonymous with giving your gift to the world. What we're talking about here is much more powerful than being a philanthropist only. You are fine tuning your uniqueness for the sake of uplifting humanity. And remember, great abundance will come through the energy of your desire to be of service. It is something miraculous about volunteering to be a servant of the Universal Kingdom, you automatically live as a king!

Although virtue is its on reward, one of its perks is that it naturally unfolds material wealth. So check your level of willingness to contribute. This is important. Whenever you are short of money or in debt, your finances are in direct proportion with the intention of your giving and how you have served. Finances can be increased quickly, but only as your soul prospers. They go hand and hand. The good news is you are in complete control of when and how this happens. It is now up to you to seize it!

Join Asha's VIP Club FREE at www.ashatyson.com for further support

CHAPTER 9

The #1 Ingredient to Success

While you're working on your passion, recognize the state of rampage we're in and how it can detain you from your goals. We all feel the heat of the blazing and bulldozing through life everybody's doing these days. People dash headfirst into combat allowing data to overwhelm them. We live on fast forward, borrowing from future sunshines, and stealing the weeks ahead of us before they actually come. Everyone's constantly skimming the scene for the Next Big Thing that pledges to get everyone working better and faster. Bottom line — we're in a hurry.

More often than not, we speed right through what we claim to care about. It shows up everywhere in life from the forgotten child left in the car, to the missed birthday of a friend. Many people aren't true to their word anymore. Making commitments lightly and consistently disappointing others appears to be the rule, rather than the exception. Even though we have buzzer, ringer and beeper sounds coming from our handbags, hips and briefcases, some are still failing to return important phone calls, show up for appointments, or even follow-up on plans they've made themselves. More communication mechanisms than ever before are at our finger tips and still folks are missing in action.

Our World Moves in Gigabytes

We now have access to the most sophisticated technology ever, but efficiency still escapes us. How many times have you tried to handle business only to hear, "The computers are down, call back?" No one seems to notice that computers being "down" isn't an excuse for not serving customers.

Ironically, it feels more like we're going backwards rather than using our developments to get ahead. In the midst of the chaos, we're losing everything more frequently—the keys, the kids, our minds, the paperwork we had just a second ago. We're checking more mail than ever before; voice mails, emails, and the good old fashion snail mail from the postmaster. And for all you do, can you say it has really put you more in control or in touch?

With over zealous schedules, our attention spans and patience levels are getting shorter as the work hours grow longer. Even a thirty-six hour day wouldn't be enough.

We're constantly buying new things, but not finding the time to organize what we already have. Responsibilities mount yet your energy isn't being replenished.

Whew! It makes one wonder, what in the world is the huge rush? Why are we so busy, and busy doing what? What are we looking for exactly? And will we even know when we've found it, if we find it? And should we find it, will it have all been worth it?

I suspect we've traded in a connection with ourselves for the sake of being "In the know." The talk that's sprayed throughout our culture says to be smarter and better you must get the new toys, get involved in all the cutting edge concepts and over commit yourself. After some time, the messages get conflictive and messy. Meanwhile we seek for the knowledge it would take to reclaim ourselves, not realizing we have it, and we've had it all the time. Without stopping to think or even breathe, we live a life of anxiety, and continue to buy into the hype that complicates our focus. In our efforts to find the magic secret—the cure, we've become unraveled.

When you're over tasked, you'll miss the answer altogether. In the midst of it all, what I know for sure is that you can't be successful stuck to the red tape. I submit to you that the most competitive advantage in this rapid society, is and always has been *order*.

Order is the number one ingredient to success.

To achieve order one must make things simple. If order is the first law of heaven, how much more important is it on earth?

The Advantages of Simplicity are Extraordinary

When your entire life has been trimmed down to what's simple, direct and lean, you harness the power to see way ahead. You tend to be centered on what really matters to you, rather than abstractly engaging in a bunch of scrambled activities. You're less likely to be absentminded or preoccupied. While everyone and everything else is zipping full force in all directions around you, make it your business to master the art and experience the value of clarity. Confusion costs, and no one can afford it. Your entire approach to living and everything concerning you must be organized and aligned for accomplishment. Nothing in your life can be muddled or unintelligible. Bring absolute order to everything you're apart of, starting with your home.

This produces tremendous trickle down action. Clearing your most intimate space will have profound affects on how everything else fits together. Purge. Eliminate. Then magnify and intensify what works well in your house. Command sense of your living quarters from wall to wall, corner to corner and within each and every section of the rooms that you are custodian of.

What our homes look like is symbolic of how we feel internally in each moment. Notice, when we are in a cleaning mood we're usually in a good place emotionally, and things are going fairly well. Some people clean while they're upset unconsciously hoping whatever's on their mind will get better as they straighten. Clearing what is deranged is a very good way to immediately participate in your own healing.

Though it is important, purifying your home is not just about buckets and soap. Seeking distinctness in your personal environment is a deep and meaningful process that will reward you spiritually, emotionally and financially.

We Live in too Much Space

We purchase, acquire, collect, accumulate and store! And it's never enough. Cutting the fat, and opening up your physical space allows you to stretch your thinking power and pull out new levels of creativity. Start by asking yourself a few questions about your present lifestyle.

Is your home and the things in your life user friendly? Do you have easy-to-access tools that help you pursue your goals without hesitation? Do your drawers open with ease or are you slightly struggling to pull them out? Do you even know what's in them? What about those closets? The kitchen cabinets? The trunk of the car? The basement or attic? Is everything functional and operative? All light fixtures have working bulbs? Are they plugged in and ready for usage?

Have you set yourself up for success?

Even at work, what about your desk? Is your filing caught

up? Now, I know filing is not likely to be a favorite task, but with knowing this, have you created a system that makes it easier to take on? The goal is to be able to put your hand on what you need inside of an amazing time frame. You set the time. Can you get anything you need in your home or workplace inside of 2 hours, 30 minutes, 15 minutes, what? It is for you to decide what's remarkable yet reasonable. Most people aren't very organized. Make it your strength.

Decluttering Down to What Makes You Smile

Nothing in your home should be something you're just tolerating or living with passively. And most certainly nothing should annoy you in your sacred palace. Get past any fear of throwing away what you think you may need one day."Pack-ratting"will postpone productivity, and after awhile, you lock yourself up inside your own maze. It isn't necessary to bring everything in the world into your home in order to have access to what you need. You have to believe in the power of global resources as well as have faith in your ability to access them. Prosperity flows through an overstocked home much like water through a clogged drain.

All items in your home should have active roles in making statements about who you are. If you don't absolutely love it or use it regularly, it doesn't belong there. Your belongings should be vibrant expressions of your inner workings. Your home must be fully equipped with things you vigorously use daily, monthly or yearly to optimize efficiency.

What clothes or shoes could go? What trinkets, objects or what-nots are you allowing to just live with you because you paid good money for them, or you feel guilty about getting rid of them because they were gifts? You have to evaluate your property to see if it helps to serve your goals. Every *thing* within the walls of your home should bring you a sense of joy when you look at it, touch it, or use it.

If any personal possession simply exists in your world without making as much as a slight contribution to your overall happiness, it can rightly be labeled "junk" and should be removed. Consider allowing someone else the opportunity to make good use of some of the things you are just holding on to. Sometimes we keep what used to work or what we hope will serve us again someday. This is energy robbing to say the least. It's necessary to live in the moment. You do this by embracing who you are right now. Buy and keep clothes, choose house decor and select and *de*select only what represents your current authentic self.

Neatness Attracts Prosperity

Keep things orderly and in designated areas. This includes receipts, memoirs, keepsakes, linen, toiletries, food and important documents. If you find it difficult to decide the pocket or heading to place your documents under in your personal filing system, make broader categories rather than small closely related ones that can cause you to second guess yourself. Where would you look first for your automobile insurance policy...under *automobile* or *insurance*? Either one is fine. Do what makes sense to your brain, then stick to it. Wherever your thoughts first take you, is where it belongs.

"But what if after I put it somewhere, the next time I go to look for it, I can't remember if I'd originally gone with automobile or insurance?"

One solution would be to give everything a home once, then memorize the address, so to speak. This means to assign all of your belongings a specific place, then acknowledge these "home assignments" as permanent from now on. This will be full proof. To ensure that you remember where the "home assignment" is, spend a few moments associating the thing with where you've placed it before you move on to something else. This is the most important part. Put things where you want them, then literally hold still long enough to mentally connect the each thing with its permanent home. You'll need to discipline yourself to do this until it becomes automatic. If you're prone to throwing things anywhere just to get them out of your way for the time being, you could very well learn to throw them in their homes. It wouldn't take much more effort especially when you consider all the benefits that come with knowing where things are. You'll avoid the frustration that builds when we aren't able to find what we need quickly.

The concept of home assigning reminds me of how visually impaired people independently function in their homes. It's fascinating how many of them know exactly where everything is. They're able to do this because all of their belongings have been placed once and they can depend on themselves to put things back where they go.

If you are not organized, realize it's costing you wealth, even if you don't see how. You may very well be functioning in the turmoil, but it won't be at your optimum peak. You simply won't create, produce or prepare for challenge as a champion soldier when you can't find your gear.

Scaling Back

Develop a passion for downsizing your life to something that makes sense to you as it also supports your goals. You should have a personal mastery of your castle. This means knowing where everything is, what everything is and how it's used. Even when a room belongs to someone else in your home, you know what it is. *It's a room that belongs to someone else!* This knowledge can bring you great liberty. Thank goodness you don't have to be concerned with how this room is kept. As long as, with a closed door, nothing falls out of it, grows out of it or generates a smell, this is one less matter you have to contend with. Enjoy the freedom!

In getting it all together, it's essential to acknowledge your unique natural tendencies. Then give yourself permission to express them. Trust your instincts. Where does your mind tell you the home office supplies go? Are they to be together in a designated place within sensible reach or is it logical to you that they live spreaded throughout the house? What about the things you love and can trust yourself to buy forever?

A good friend of mine adores jewelry, mainly earrings. At one point, she had them everywhere. Her nightstand drawers were filled, several jewelry boxes had long been maxed out. More were in the master bath, and quite a few formed a trail haphazardly throughout the house. What was she suppose to do? Stop buying them? I think not. To discontinue experiencing the joy earrings brought her was not the answer.

We need to do more of what tickles our spirit, not less. Earrings had clearly become more than jewelry to her. They were small pieces of precious art—tokens of her self expression. This is what she loved. This type of partiality is nothing to feel guilty or inconvenienced about; in fact we should celebrate when we make discoveries about ourselves. The first step was to gather all her earrings together in one place. The second step was to contain them.

Containing is the part that eludes us. If they don't sell anything in the stores that suit our needs, we can very easily make the mistake of altering our lifestyles to fit what's available, rather than making available what fits our individual lifestyles. Understand that manufacturers play to the masses for profit and gain. Consequently, our individual needs get lost in the shuffle and fall through the cracks. We buy into the illusion that we're somehow dysfunctional misfits who need to correct ourselves in order to fit the mold. It's then that you must be mindful of the truth.

The truth is, we are the real works of art, magnificent in every way, and it's the mold that needs adjusting. I was shopping for boots which had always been a challenge. The top part of the boots are usually too large for my calves. This particular time, several shoppers were sitting nearby as I was trying on boots. One lady said:

"I have the opposite problem, honey; my leg is too big for the top of the boot, and I have to force the zipper up!"Someone else said:

"All she needs to do is stuff um with leg warmers." Finally, a third woman told me:

"Just eat more and then come back!"

It was then I realized these were the kind of aristocratic conversations throughout our entire lives that convince us we're the ones who are broken or flawed. The messages throughout our culture tells us to deal with discomforts and just accept that it doesn't get any better. We aren't affirmed in our entitlement to be accommodated for who we are, but when you are grounded in self love, you understand that you deserve, even when it isn't of popular opinion. Here, the boots had been made by "man," while my leg had been created by God. Who dare say it is God who needs to go back to the drawing board?

Customize to Your Uniqueness

Join Asha's VIP Club FREE at www.ashatyson.com for further support

Be prepared to design what you need from scratch. The fact that no one has thought of selling or even making what you need doesn't take from the valuable impact it can have on your life. We had never seen a jewelry unit that would accommodate my friend's lifestyle, but that didn't mean she was to settle for what was being sold. She simply would have to design a jewelry closet that favored her growing earring wardrobe.

Perhaps she needed an entire room or even a whole wing in her home just for earrings! Nothing is unreasonable when you're talking about doing what will work for your life. This is about making your domain your very own.

Whatever you have, group like items together, then contain them. If you have hundreds or thousands of music cd's, you may need to contract a carpenter; apparently, you have a love for music beyond the average person. Therefore, you need a unit that is beyond what is being designed for the average cd owner.

If you love books, rather than have them scattered all over the house, bring them together and decide what will be suitable. Maybe at one point a shelf with a couple of book ends was fine. With time, a five shelf bookcase worked well. Perhaps you now have what constitutes a full fledge library where bookshelves should be serving as your wallpaper!

The idea is to move from inertia and fuel your productivity power by getting your house in order. As mentioned before, it's necessary to bring order to every aspect of your life.

In addition to your home and work space, you must organize your doings and undertakings as well. Is your time spent orderly or complicated? It's essential to arrange your priorities and your endeavors if success is your goal.

*Join Asha's VIP Club FREE at **www.ashatyson.com** for further support*

Are You Doing Too Much?

Do you know anyone who is always involved in a zillion different projects, but still hasn't achieved the level of success they want? They appear to be spinning their wheels.

There's someone I've known for a while who is smart and enthusiastic about life, but he has so many occupations that he gets tangled in his own dream. At one point he'd served as a barber, a minister, a poet, a hospital orderly, a mortgage broker and a jewelry maker all at the same time! Typically, it's the multi-talented who get caught in this "jack of all trade" webbing.

Sometimes you might feel things would be easier if your gift were clear cut. Then you wouldn't have to search for it; it would just jump out at you. People who can only sing, sing. People who can only paint, paint. They're good at what they do, and it makes it a little easier for them to enhance that one talent. Besides that, our society rewards single talents. As consumers, we spend our dollars where we know the product or service we're paying for is the merchant's specialty; we simply want the best, and for us that means single focus. Most of us wouldn't patronize a business that answered the company phone saying:

"Squeaky's used cars, barbecue, dog grooming and video; hold please."

This sounds like a place that does any and everything to make a dollar. We would believe it is a non-reputable hustle—not a business of any specific expertise. Imagine Hershey's Chocolate suddenly starting to manufacture hair spray. We wouldn't want to hear of such a thing!

So to our friend who does it all, please know when there are too many irons in the fire something is going to burn up. There is an old Chinese proverb that says, "When you chase two rabbits they'll both escape!" It's possible to have it all, you can use your multi-talents to create mini-profit centers, but you must pace yourself wisely.

Pacing Yourself When You're Multi-talented

So what's a person to do when they are endowed with several talents? What if you have leadership skills, stage performing qualities, administrative abilities, while also being able to design wall murals, rebuild carburetors, and bake New York style cheesecake that brings the rich and famous to their knees!

The key here is to rank and position your special gifts systematically making them all inclusive in your life. But where do you start? Which do you do first and when?

Sometimes when we don't have these answers, we find ourselves scurrying around aimlessly doing too much, too little or nothing at all. This is what I call "talent palsy." The brain gives a directive, but the body won't go. It's frustrating to have a vision of what your life could be, while seemingly unable to take the necessary steps to get there. So what is our talented friend to do with the leadership skills, stage performing qualities, administrative abilities and all that other stuff?

First, make a list of the talents. Then, while also considering where she ultimately wants to go in life, organize the gifts in such a way they'll take her there.

Perhaps she could rebuild carburetors to generate cash in order to move to New York. There she could use her administrative skills to start her own business supplying cheesecake to restaurants and grocers. After earning start-up capital from sales, she could then open her own cheesecake cafe. To create the perfect cosmopolitan atmosphere, naturally her own artwork would be the logical choice. On the walls of her shoppe, she could design the ambience of a serene seaside terrace that keeps her customers returning repeatedly. Who knows what opportunities will result from show-casing her work? Meanwhile, the success of her growing business now begs the need for employees. Here is where she gets to demonstrate her leadership skills by hiring a sharp team who will execute premier customer service while she's out. Out where, you say? Out strengthening and auditioning her stage performing qualities for what may be her big break on Broadway!

Getting on the Move!

And so you see, you have to move in your splendor by getting and staying creative and hopeful. Motionlessness serves no one; be smart as you keep moving in the direction of your dream. "What use is a good head if the legs won't carry it?"

Stagnation can also come from needing to do things perfectly. And too the perfectionist, I submit this for consideration: No one knows what you're actually capable of. The notch below what you thought the task required is usually beyond what the average person had in mind anyway. So whatever you do will be good enough—that is if you get around to doing it. My guess is, it's not the mistakes you've made in life that keeps you stopped as much as it's the fear of making new ones. But as we've established, we can't accomplish anything allowing fear to hold us back.

If you're overwhelmed by your many talents, take note of all you would like to do and are capable of, be sure to avoid judging your circumstances or debating with yourself about whether or not doing this thing is possible. Right now, only think about what your catalog of abilities are. Next, connect the dots.

Which one of your talents could you singlemindedly focus on first as if it were the only thing you were good at? Perhaps this is your favorite interest or the one you do most frequently. It may be a hobby and not what you currently earn money for. Explore the depths of this skill you have. Have you seen anyone else become successful doing it or doing something similar? Is it ground breaking, yet needed? Are you fairly certain you would do well whether anyone else has done it or not?

Disregard the negativity people may attach to your mission. Yours is to stay committed to the possibilities of your life. Where is there a need? What are people discussing? Stay focused and groom your first skill aggressively. Study. Get hungry about knowledge, but be very careful not to get stuck at being a "book worm"or a"self-help junkie."Make sure you get around to doing your craft and not just learning and reading about it.

Next, determine how the talent you've honed can be used to fill the needs of people. After you feel comfortable with that particular proficiency, gradually link and rope in your other gifts. This will expand your ability to reach more people and fill more voids. Be sure to think on paper. Write out your talent merging strategy, list your objectives, and get some idea of who will benefit from your aptitude. The goal is to feel challenged and fulfilled as you use up all your stuff. Be patient with yourself, this procedure requires distinct concentration.

Concentrate

I never understood the expression, "Don't put all your eggs in one basket."

Why not?

Here again we have one of those trite sayings derived from tradition that doesn't support success. It's basically telling us to sprinkle our eggs everywhere in case we fail, then we'll have something to fall back on. It tells you to have doubt about achieving your ultimate life's dream. That way, when it doesn't pan out, and it probably won't based on this advice, you'll have a surplus of substitute dreams in a garage somewhere like spare tires.

I like what Andrew Carnegie says: "Real concentration is to put all your eggs in one basket, then watch that basket." Remember, we get the situations in life we set up for. Scattered eggs undermine success and demonstrates uncertainty at the very beginning. I maintain, if you're skeptical about your abilities to do your first goal, it's the same as accepting something secondary right out the gate. Thomas Edison leaves us with this: "I had learned from years of experience with people, that when a person desires a single thing so deeply that she is willing to stake her entire future on a single turn of the wheel in order to get it, she is sure to win!"

Consider Brandy; actress, singer and model. She's a wonderful example of a person who is just as good at one thing as she is another. Look at how she demonstrated her many talents. Brandy took her time and paced her talents wisely and first became established as a professional actress. Later we learned not only could she act, she could sing with extraordinary ability. The confidence she has exhibited in her talents is so incredible that she strategically maintains her notoriety in each skill independently. Notice, Moesha, the character Brandy plays on the sitcom *Moesha*, can't sing at all. In fact, certain episodes stress this exclusively by allowing her to pretend she's not capable of singing. This reminds the viewer, Brandy doesn't have to sing to act nor does she have to act to sing. This has earned her well deserved places in both industries.

So, organize your house, your thoughts, your talents, your work, your life. Purging, containing, and talent connecting will all require some creativity and concentration, but it's worth it, and I know you can do it. Get your affairs in order from top to bottom and tie all loose ends. Keep in mind, when you erase the chaos, the vision you have for your life will become sharper, clearer and closer by the minute!

CHAPTER 10

Money

If you've been tempted to skip ahead to this chapter, I recommend you reconsider. It's highly unlikely you will gain what's needed starting here. Also, might I suggest, if it's freedom and wealth you want, but you don't have time to read an entire book on assessing it, it's a good idea to *re*evaluate your priorities.

I do understand why there would be eagerness to get to this chapter. Here I discuss money—plain and simple. Many don't often have enough because they focus intensively on lack. Out of the fear of not having comes a constant and compulsive intent on getting more—more stuff, more nice things, more money. It's this ever revolving cycle of dollar chasing that keeps us behind prosperity.

Seeking the money first is to put the cart before the horse. To change the outer condition of anything in your life, you must first change the inner condition. Many think if only they had more money they wouldn't be down and discouraged. Please know: we're never depressed because we're broke; we're broke because we're depressed. It's important to know that if money is deficient in your life, it's the effect of an existing emotional issue; and not the cause of one. The lack of money is simply the result of other unresolved emotional issues. If you're short of funds, one way or another somewhere in your life, you've accepted the falsehood of limitation.

Whatever belief you have that has you blocked right now, will have to change before you will be able to tap into your infinite bank account.

Can You Stand to Be Rich?

We have several criticisms and prejudices against money that can keep us from being honest, even with ourselves, so rather than to break down and defeat these deeply embedded beliefs that don't serve financial growth, we make excuses for why we're broke. You'll never have more money than what you believe is possible, so you have to get honest here. Ask yourself the question, "Do I want to be rich?" Ironically, it's rare to find people who are brave enough to admit to wanting lots of money. Most people are afraid or ashamed to claim they want to be financially wealthy because of all the bad publicity money gets.

On any given day you could ask several people simply this: "Do you want to be rich?" Almost never will you get a simple "yes." Instead, they will rattle off a long philosophical answer about how being rich doesn't make you happy, and can't buy love. Then they usually drive their point home by reciting all the names of the rich and famous people who committed suicide.

So, what is this person really saying? Are they telling us that they have strategically avoided wealth because they don't want to risk being more unhappy or even suicidal as a result of having money?

Where is the logic in this belief?

I contend that some elements of this belief are true, money

can't buy happiness or love. But who ever said it could? Let's keep money in perspective. Money is simply a tool that gives you access to what is likely a better life for you and yours. It makes life more convenient. Money is merely a tangible way for us to trade. However, I don't think the real issue for our "Money don't buy happiness"philosopher is about buying love. I believe that the talk they do is simply an act of "smoke and mirrors" in order to avoid facing the real truth—*feelings of unworthiness and/or jealousy.*

For this person, it somehow feels gratifying to think that rich people are miserable even with "all that money." Believing this, consoles their own financial inadequacies, thus making their personal struggle easier to take. Please understand I do recognize it is not necessary to be financially wealthy to be happy. What I am recommending is that you be honest with yourself about whether or not you are purposely repelling wealth for a higher call—as people who have taken vows of poverty—or simply making excuses for being broke. Using puffed up philosophy to justify lack will draw lack all the more. Be truthful with yourself. After all, who says you can't be both happy and rich? The answer is: No one said it. It is our philosopher who would rather not believe that money and happiness can go together. If they believed the two could go together, they would have to question why they really haven't achieved?

No, not every rich person is happy, but there are many who are. Why not focus on the possibility of being one of them?

Are You Sure Money Isn't Everything?

"Money isn't everything," is another popular chant. This one is not altogether true. Money is absolutely everything when you don't have any! It consumes you and preoccupies you with it's whereabouts. When there's a financial need pressing before you, there isn't usually any room for another thought. Your primary concentration is on how to cover that check or send in that payment. All of your time, efforts and energy go into making ends meet, arguing with bill collectors, and just getting by. Let's face it; it's hard work being poor. It's costly mentally, spiritually, emotionally, and physically. When you are stressed and worried, you can't begin to see what else, if anything matters at all. In this regard money becomes everything.

When asked "Do you want to be rich?" Some say "Not really." Should you ask them why not, they say, they just want to be "comfortable." Or they use some other vague terming like "well off" or "content." The only problem with this is we can't attain an unspecified, fuzzy financial goal. How much is "well-off?" And what exactly does "comfortable"mean? This belief comes with an "I-could-be-rich-if-I-wanted-to-but-I-don't-need-much-so-I'm-not" attitude. "I don't need all that," they say. And for a few people this is probably the case. Rich can mean different things to different people. But again, be honest with yourself and make sure that the belief isn't a justification for being broke.

A Carefree Life is a Rich One No Matter How You Slice it

You can't limit abundance. Prosperity just doesn't work that way. It's a free flowing energy that doesn't have a gage switch. It's either welcome into your life or it isn't. It's like an electrical outlet. You're either plugged into it or you're not.

You don't get to tell the energy source how much it should be piping through. Besides, while the money is coming, who would really say, "Okay, money you can slow down now because if you keep coming in bulk like this I'll become a rich person, and I'm only interested in being comfortable!"

Energy doesn't distinguish and sort through all the hang-ups, and discriminations people have about money. It just passes that person by and goes to someone who declares with conviction that they are rich in consciousness and are ready, willing and able to be rich in unlimited manifestation. It is based on this premise that the rich do, in fact, get richer. The rich have learned how to be accepting of bountifulness. They are money magnets who are open and receptive to the privileges of living well; while people who try to regulate prosperity are usually the ones that are spending their money long before it's earned.

God and Rich People

Another success robbing myth is the belief that being financially wealthy is not pleasing to God. Someone once told me these words: "God don't like rich people too much." Misinterpretations of biblical teachings have convinced many that the wealthy are greedy, materialistic and ungodly. The truth is, rich folks aren't necessarily anti-spiritual and poor people aren't necessarily holy. What's unholy is when we deviate from expressions of love. And everyone is capable of doing that regardless of bank account balances.

Also, we have often heard the misquote, "Money is the root of all evil." When accurately quoted it actually states that the "*love* of money is the root of all evil." Let's be clear. The denotation of the word *love* means *worship* in this instance. And yes, to worship money leads to destruction. However, to love the *Source* of money is the key to all prosperity. We don't love money. We love the Source of it. God is the Source. Again, money is simply a tool He uses for helping us keep score for what has and what hasn't been accumulated in our material world. That's it. Money is not power, love, or anything deep. Money itself is not good, bad, right or wrong. It's nothing. It's how money is used that assigns its virtue.

What Do You Believe?

There are several possible beliefs. But the question is, what are yours and does it serve you in getting what you want out of life? We know that when you hold on to poverty through your consciousness, you attract its physical demonstration in your life. In order to improve the quality of what you attract, it's necessary to believe something different in your soul's chief council chamber. Check in. What false truths could you have in the recesses of your mind? Do you believe "It takes money to make money?"And so, if you don't have any money you're just out of luck? We understand some endeavors require money to make some. Then fine, make some. Earn it. After all, the money is there!

There is Plenty of Money for You!

The physical presence of money is plentiful, there's more than enough of it to go around for everybody and it can be relatively easy to obtain. Let's say you invented something to improve the quality of people's lives. The price of your product is only one dollar. Most people have a dollar, even children. Or if you are in Canada of course most people have a "loonie."

Now suppose we were going to market this item in Michigan where there are nine million residents. If everybody bought your merchandise, you would have nine million dollars at the end of your trip!

"But Asha, everybody's not going to buy."

This is true; some people won't take what's good for them for free. So, let's grossly reduce your customers by half. With only half of the state purchasing your goods, you would have to live off four and a half million dollars! You poor thing. How about being even more reserved with our optimism? What if only half of that half bought into your idea? What would you have? Two and a quarter million, right? You still aren't in the unemployment line. Now let's be obsessively conservative, and cut it in half for the final time. You still walk away with well over one million dollars! And please keep in mind, you never left the state of Michigan, hardly anybody bought and yet you've achieved financial wealth!

Imagine if you were to take your product or service and expand your marketing efforts to the other states, some of which are larger than Michigan! What if your product or service had been priced at more than one dollar?

As practicing consumers, we've all bought something for more than one dollar—a blouse, a kitchen appliance, a video game, a meal—something. So we're going to make a price adjustment. Your commodity is in great demand now. It no longer costs the customer just a buck; it's now five dollars. How about ten or even fifty? Look at that math!

So, we know that wealth is accessible, and no one can take your share. We have the technology and the resources such that every person on the planet could live like a millionaire! All you have to do is get resourceful; get persistent; get creative. Think. Talk to people, listen to people, do your homework, learn, get hungry for wisdom and get desperate for understanding. These are the things required to change your life. So, get busy!

That is the beauty in being who you are and in being human. No one can put a cap on your imagination; therefore, you can always explore the options and the potential of infinite possibilities. Your power allows you to choose and *re*choose at any given moment, so choose to believe that you will always have what you need if you just stay in the game. Don't give up. Despite any opposition, nothing is more certain than the success of a person with a made up mind. Believe me on this; if your passion to press forward with your project, task, program, or whatever your mission outweighs any obstacle, financial or otherwise, you can't and you won't be denied. You have to move forward with the core stance that what you're doing must be done. Believe within yourself that this has to happen! And money, least of all, will not stop me. You'll be surprised what having that attitude will release for you. When you believe this with conviction, Accessing money will never be difficult again.

Discover How Great it is To be You

Do you think you need a name or reputation to write your luxury ticket? Have you ever said, "It's not what you know but who you know?" Would things have been better if you were a Vanderbilt, Rockefeller, or Getty? If so, be prepared to rethink your beliefs.

Although family inheritance is thought to be a common way for becoming wealthy, in reality, 80% of this country's super rich are first generation millionaires. So it really doesn't matter where you start or where you come from. Most people have built wealth from scratch!

I acknowledge that any influence in your favor will be helpful, but ultimately it will have to be *you* who shapes and molds *your* place in prosperity. Knowing "somebody" is a supplement to *what* you know. *Who* you know may get you to the stage, but *what* you know will keep you there. "Networking" has it's place, but it doesn't take the place of polished talent. Don't be misled, people are very smart. We always know when a person has allowed themselves to be manufactured through nepotism, favoritism, name-dropping, "brown-nosing and elbow-rubbing. Rather spend your time doing the things that make a name for yourself rather than trying to meet someone who has made one for themselves. Besides, not knowing anyone can have its advantages.

Some people find it positively refreshing to see an ambitious, old fashioned self-starter who is well prepared, has good intentions and tremendous drive. These qualities far outweigh connections every time.

Are You Repelling Wealth?

It seems that rejecting wealth is prevalent in our country. I was once asked by an organization to do a very unusual but fascinating exercise immediately after keynoting their special event. This client wanted me to help each audience member determine their core beliefs as to why they weren't realizing their financial goals. The people there were eager to unveil the hidden reasons why they were in the way of themselves. None of them had achieved the financial success they desired. Interesting enough, all of the wealth rejecting beliefs found that day were simple yet destructive.

One lady discovered that beneath all the success she claimed to want, was the fear of being sued. Her dream was to be a cartoonist. She had created characters and drafted a comic book, which by the way was prepared well enough to sell. She said her characters resembled some other famous cartoon, so she believed the company that had the rights to those characters would definitely sue her.

Her biggest fear in life was court. She was terrified by the idea of court so severely that the thought of it made her physically ill. She had sworn to herself she would never be in another situation that could lead to court as did her nasty divorce.

As far fetched and impractical as all of this may seem to us, it's enough to detour a very intelligent person from wealth if they really believe it. Despite the fact that she told herself and the world that she wanted to be a cartoonist, it had been her fear based belief that really governed her choices and said otherwise. Since you can't make money doing things that you never get around to doing, this would be a classic case of repelling wealth.

This person had a dream she allowed to turn into a nightmare by the power of her thoughts alone. In her mind, she had already become a successful cartoonist who was taken to court, got sick, lost the case and resigned from life a failure.

Another audience member uncovered truth for himself when he admitted that he was deeply afraid of paying taxes. He said the more money he made the more he had to pay. Hence, the less money he made, the less Uncle Sam would take.

He had subconsciously denied earning his fortune in order to protect it from the government! The notion of taxes taking a toll on his financial bonanza was more dreadful to him than never having wealth at all!

However, what he shows the world and tells himself is that he is looking to earn as much money as possible for his family. All the while, his soul's belief is urging him to resist higher tax brackets. Completely unaware of his actions, he had been sabotaging his own success by procrastinating and making excuses for why promotions and salary increases weren't happening.

At the heart of another woman's secret truth was the belief that she simply wasn't smart enough. She believed she wasn't smart enough to earn or maintain large sums of money. She thought rich people where extra brilliant and somehow had special insight she didn't and couldn't have.

It's human nature to want to avoid looking ridiculous or stupid. We have a tendency to move away from things and areas we don't understand. Her self preserving strategy was this: If I don't have any money, no one smarter than me will be able to trick me out of my fortune. Also, by blending in with other financial strugglers, she could safely be out of the spotlight and avoid being scorned and questioned about her success.

Then there was the woman who feared earning more than her husband. She had been raised with traditional values and associated power and bread winning with masculinity. Her core belief was that being wealthy would compromise her femininity and make her less attractive to her companion. She said that although he told her he wouldn't be threatened by her earning more than him, she had over heard him saying the opposite on many occasions. She found that her deeply embedded truth had been causing her to resist opportunities for financial advancement.

Remember, these kinds of self destructive beliefs are not usually on the surface of your consciousness. Also, it doesn't matter how ridiculous the belief seems to someone else. If it's your truth, it will rule.

How Do You Respond to Money Matters?

It is necessary to pay attention to how you think about money. Are you optimistic, positive and hopeful or do you find yourself feeling overwhelmed, negative and burdened? If you aren't thrilled with your income level, ask yourself, "What do I *really* believe, and what has my self-talk been about? Ask yourself whether or not you have bought into any of the pre existing money myths or perhaps ones you've created for yourself? Remember any belief that doesn't promote prosperity will obstruct prosperity no matter how trivial it seems. So be willing to examine all your opinions about money. Do you really feel worthy of financial success?

Our impulse response to this question is usually a resounding "yes." But how would the inner most part of your being answer? Consider these things. Do you spend more money on others than you do yourself? Do you ever feel guilty buying for yourself when you have children? What about the "good stuff?"Do you save the "good stuff" for special occasions? You know, the "good towels" and the "good dishes?" I never quite understood why as a child I was not allowed in the living room. We only used it when we had company. That didn't make a great deal of sense to me. How could only visitors be allowed in the *living* room when they didn't even *live* there? Check your worthiness factor. Do you find that you favor others at your own expense?

What I am suggesting is that if you don't have as much money as you need or want, somewhere, somehow, on some level of your conscious or subconscious mind, you are rejecting abundance and repelling wealth. What darkness is lurking in your deeper consciousness? It's important to find out what's holding you back from what you deserve. Does the face you show the world and the things you say both to yourself and to others match your true soul's belief? If not, it will undoubtedly affect your relationship with money. So it's time to find the seed beliefs that have governed your finances until now.

Locate a quiet environment where you'll be free from distraction for one solid hour. It may take less time. But please don't panic if it takes longer. Have a pen and paper ready. Meditate. Pray for clarity before doing this exercise believing you'll have understanding. Sit straight but comfortable and relaxed with your eyes closed and your mind open. Prepare to be informed and expect to fully understand what you're about to experience. Focus intently, and while using the power of your visualization, envision holding a twenty dollar bill in your hands. See it clearly. What does it feel like? Is it crumpled or crisp? Is the bill old with a small Jackson or new with the enlargement? Allow this money to represent all the money you've ever had. Should you find it difficult to hold the image in your mind, feel free to use real money. Imagine it's a living being that's capable of complimenting you, complaining about you, or anything else someone could do who has been in a long term relationship with you. If money could talk, and you were to ask it questions, how would it respond? With these things in mind, please prepare for the exercise on the next page.

Instructions: You are asking your money the following questions; pretend it is able to answer you back. After you've asked, be sure to write down the very first answer that comes to your mind before moving on to the next question. For best results, avoid skipping questions and be honest with yourself by embracing the truest answer. The most authentic answer will be the first one that comes to you. Let's begin.

- **Money, during the course of our relationship what has my attitude been towards you?**

- **Money, do I love you? If so, why?**

- **Money, am I afraid of you? If so, why?**

- **On a scale from 1 to 10 how would you measure my honesty regarding you specifically?**
  (You will instantaneously see a number in your mind; write it down.)

- **Money, if you are running from me, what things do I say or do in particular that perpetuate this situation?**

Review your answers. Once you know what your disposition is with finances, you'll know what changes to make. Be sure to ask God to heal you from any ill feelings about money. Do this exercise as often as you wish. You'll find that your answers change as you continue to do your soulwork. Undoubtedly, you are on your way to developing a better relationship with money.

Prepare for Wealth

We will only draw into our lives the situations we're ready for. Have you ever heard someone say, "I knew it wasn't going to work out, that's why I didn't bother." But what they didn't understand is that they didn't bother, and that's why it didn't work out. They set themselves up from the start and got what they anticipated. So now you must invite money into your life. How you do that is by expecting and looking forward to your wealth. Get prepared for it.

Organize your debts. Never leave your bills tucked away, hidden and unopened. OPEN THEM. Coordinate them with the envelopes creditors have provided. Get rid of duplicate bills; keep only the most recent ones regarding each account. As new ones come, throw old ones out. Place stamps on all of your unsealed envelopes. You won't be mailing them until you have the money, which is coming, but you are preparing for the situation you expect. Get busy; start moving and allow energy to flow. Shake things up and stir some stuff around. Proactively demonstrate with your mind, body and soul that you're making some changes around here. And that new and exciting things are about to happen!

Request a copy of your consumer credit report from all three major bureaus—Experian (formally TRW) 1-888-397-3742, Transunion 1-800-916-8800 and Equifax 1-800-658-1111. It's important to get all three because some creditors only report to one or two different bureaus. You need to know what everybody is saying about how you pay your bills. If there are mistakes on them such as bills that have been paid but are showing up unpaid; accounts you've never had are on the report or any other thing that is suspect at all, fix it. Stay persistent with the creditors and the bureaus about making corrections. If you need to explain a circumstance regarding some things that are on the report to potential creditors, exercise your right to include a personal statement that will be attached to your credit reports. To learn more about repairing your credit, read books and identify resources that deal with consumer credit repair specifically. If you don't live in the United States, find out what you need in order to evaluate your credit where you live. This is an important step in your financial recovery. You must pay everyone you owe. Otherwise, you interfere with the flow of abundance. When you maintain outstanding debt, you detain your own prosperity. If you're withholding someone's funds for whatever reason, someone else will withhold yours. This goes for all creditors—organizations as well as individuals. As we're all very familiar, "You reap what you sow." And in this instance I use this quote as it relates to the reciprocity principle. In other words, you get back on your plate what you have indeed dished out. It doesn't matter if you have a good excuse for not having the money; the prosperity law still works. It doesn't factor in good explanations, it just rewards production. Design a financial plan and stick with it. Realize how you got here and unlike the past, deal with emotional issues separate from your finances. Be careful not to shop to feel better. Feel better to feel better. *Retail therapy* isn't the answer. Get courageous about confronting you money matters.

Pull Out Your Own Financial Skeletons

Make a list of every single soul you owe—personal loans included. Figure out to the nearest penny how much debt you're in? Begin turning the wheels by taking personal responsibility for your bills.

Start communicating with creditors and making arrangements to get inside of integrity with them by paying off the debts. If you need help with your plan, identify a reputable credit counseling service in your area that can negotiate your obligations down to something that both you and the creditor will be happy with. Often times these kinds of organizations can help you freeze the interest that's piling up as well as restore your credit rating. Be patient with yourself and again, remember how this all happened. What exactly were you trying to buy? If you were to evaluate your life back then, did you really want the *things* or the *feelings* you thought the purchases would bring? This doesn't mean beat down on yourself. You are merely going to study history so not to repeat it.

So, be gentle and compassionate with you. Most of us have been there at one time or another. We know that extenuating circumstances happen. Jobs can be lost, illnesses can strike, the death of bread-winners can devastate a household, but you'll never be issued a challenge you can't handle. You will never get more in life than what you can actually tolerate. Just sometimes you have to search out ways to get more creative about finding solutions for what's before you. The key is to (a), stay focused on solving and (b), get extra grateful for what is going right rather than complaining or being guest of honor at a pity party. You are a resolution finding and solution making machine! If I'm wrong, then tell me, how did you get this far?

Taming the Money Monster

It's difficult to face debt especially when it feels as though nothing can be done right away. Also, we often over exaggerate the size of the money monster. But now you want to get real and operate from truth. How much money is needed to free you from debt entirely? Your bills should be pulled together, labeled and designated in one place, orderly and controlled. A good Samaritan stranger should be able to walk into your house, go directly to your debts, inside of one minute make sense of your bills, then pay everything you owe without anyone's help. But when your debts are scattered and disorganized, mixed with some receipts and partial statements, combined with a little bit of what might have been paid, no one could clearly do you this favor without stressing themselves out. No one's likely to sort through piles of stuff that's everywhere in order to determine what needs to happen to free you from debt. It's simply too discouraging. And so it is with you. When you have an unsettled mess before you that looks insurmountable, you aren't motivated to go through it all either. So make it simple and clean.

Sharpen Your Visualization Skills

Get Ready!!! Get ready to see yourself inside of the prosperity you desire. Really get in there and live that reality. Don't let this visualization exercise go until you have evaluated what wealth would look like in your life. Do this daily, and visualize as many areas of your life as you can think of. What would work look like with more money? Same job? What would relationships look like? Same people? New friends? What would playtime, nap time or even the common cold look like? How do you dress now? Where do you shop for groceries, furniture, bathroom tissue? What is the design of your checkbook? Floral patterns, super heroes, outdoor scenery? Leather case, vinyl, a loose leaf binder? What? How does a trip to the bank feel now? Do you have the same banker? If you have children how does your wealth impact their lives at home and school? How does it change you emotionally, spiritually, physically? What about a visit to the doctor? Same one? New car? What kind? A pet? Buy a new house, rent a penthouse, remodel an old house? What? Get inside your new life and sharpen the image of its reality.

Everything about life as you know it will need to be evaluated using the new belief that you are worthy and capable of unlimited wealth. Once you have done that—and it may take months, be patient with yourself; it's worth it. You are worth it! You may begin to feel physical discomfort while considering some of the areas in your life as it relates to wealth. Do you get headaches, lower back pain, or stressed during certain parts of the visualization exercises? Do you get sleepy? Many times we sleep to escape the things we don't want to face in or lives. So, we resign to the bed. Hone in on any anxiety you might feel. And connect any discomfort with the thoughts you're having in the moment. Don't dismiss your natural instincts. This is how you find what's within yourself that stagnates your money flow. I will warn you; the most subtle beliefs can actually be the biggest culprits. Pay very close attention to your thoughts and the resistances that accompany them.

Learn Money

Study money. Become acquainted and comfortable with how it works. And don't allow yourself to be overwhelmed with the many financial products out there. Rise to the challenge of knowing the difference between a mutual fund and a money market account, a stock and a bond, a 401k and a 403b. Learn how to save. The biggest mistake people make regarding saving is they try to have something leftover to tuck away for themselves after paying everybody else. This is backwards. Pay yourself first (If you're a tither, pay yourself second); it's best for everyone involved in your finances. When you have made the proper investment for yourself up front, there tends to be more available for your other commitments. How? Saving builds confidence and frees you from the intensity of worry. Your energy can then be used to see additional creative ways to earn and access more money with less effort!

Learning money is especially beneficial for those with similar beliefs to the woman mentioned earlier who didn't feel smart enough to be rich. Grasp, at least, a basic understanding of money matters and it'll build your confidence. Attend personal finance workshops and read books that have easy-to-follow formats that are written in layman's terms. Even if you don't intend to invest in the stock market, have a general idea of how it works. If you don't enjoy reading, remember most recent books are on audio cassette. Watch CNBC. It's okay if you don't understand what they're talking about. Use it to familiarize yourself with financial terminology. Contact the National Association of Investment Clubs to learn about investment clubs and how to join, strengthen or start one. Their number is (248) 583-6242. If clubbing isn't your thing, and you would rather go it alone, call the American Association of Individual Investors at (312) 280-0170. The main thing to keep in mind is that you don't have to be intimidated by money. Comprehending the fundamentals of finances will be both rewarding and encouraging. And believe me there is hope for everybody!

There was a time in my life, that had someone handed me one million dollars in cash, I wouldn't have known what to do with it. I knew that FDIC only insured up to one-hundred thousand dollars. I couldn't imagine that people with more money than one-hundred thousand were putting it all in one bank and risking their fortunes. Keeping track of a bunch of bank statements from a lot of different banks seemed complicated and impractical. So what in the world were people doing who had as much as ten million, fifty million or even one-hundred million! It was all so overwhelming to me. But while remembering there are no stupid questions, I went to a bank, asked to speak to someone and shared my concerns. What I learned there would change my life forever. The insurance covers up to one-hundred thousand dollars not for each bank but rather each and every bank account that is held in a separate capacity! It was in that moment I realized I had repelled wealth in part because I feared not knowing where to put it. With this information came liberation, and now I was on my way!

What to Do When the Money Comes

Please recognize that any money you receive is not yours. You have been made temporary steward over what has always and will always belong to God. Prepare yourself to receive wealth graciously, gratefully and responsibly. Always share. To hoard will stop the flow. If you were to ball up a dollar bill and enclose it into a tight fist, nothing can fall out of your hand. But notice, nothing can come in either. But please be mindful that you must also be willing to receive.

There are some people who won't let you give them anything ever. They take exceptional pride in assuming the attitude of self sacrifice in order to win favor and come off as rock solid saints. They never need anything or anybody. Many times we think of these people as unselfish and generous because all they do is give. But they never want anything. And at the onset this seems quite honorable, but the truth is they unknowingly hurt themselves by always saying "no thank you." This is where *Receiving* gets a bad rap. Because not all acts of receiving are self-centered or inconsiderate. And when you aren't a willful and gracious receiver, it blocks your own good fortune. Constantly turning away gifts, support, or resources throws off the equilibrium of prosperity. And in all that we do, we must have balance. So participate in both giving and receiving, it's a must for success.

Earlier I mentioned that we should always share. This doesn't mean allow yourself to feel used. Giving should feel voluntary and ungoverned. Giving should feel good. If it doesn't, examine the situation. When giving, be careful not to let others determine and define how and when you share. In other words, give your resources in a way that is meaningful to you. The act of sharing is sacred and spiritual. How you do that has to be your personal choice.

After remodeling recently, I donated most of the previous furniture to a worthy charity that helps restore homes of house fire victims. As the organization was picking up the stuff, I got a phone call. The caller was a healthy, employed, socially advantaged person who was upset with me for not considering her as a candidate for the furniture. But please understand, there's a huge difference between giving from your heart where you feel there's a need versus someone trying to take something for nothing. Benevolence has to be an uninhibited act from both the giving and receiving ends. There should be no strings attached whatsoever. Charity is pure and should be based on the properties of love, trust and commitment, not from conditions of guilt, manipulation or obligation. Enjoy giving. Enjoy receiving. And let no one dictate for you the particulars of either one.

My prayer is that this book has reaffirmed your worthiness, your specialness, your brilliance—you. The strategies here aren't presented as a cure all. My intention is merely to share what has and continues to help me experience an awesome life. And I hope it has inspired, informed or empowered you. Remember, there is absolutely no reason you can't start living your best life right now as though the past doesn't matter because really it doesn't. After all, it's gone.

Act out of vision rather than react to circumstances; navigate your life by making fresh healthy choices instead of allowing stale disappointments of the past to hold you back; create dramatic increases in your effectiveness, efficiency and adaptability to make things happen no matter what else is going on.

Overcome the weaknesses that block you from your better self. Withdraw from participating in limitation and commit to possibility. Gird yourself with the armor that allows you to "act as though it is impossible to fail."And it is. Because all things work purposefully to bring you to the person you were meant to be. Review your commitments regularly. They are much like nursing home residents; if they aren't visited often they'll soon pass away. And always move towards your goals. Sometimes we move faster than others and other times we barely move at all, but you're going to be okay as long as you just keep moving! Above all, stay prayerful and trust your instincts. You my friend, will achieve success of supernatural proportions—and I'll see ya!

Other Works by Asha Tyson

It's Your Turn!

A step-by-step workbook to accessing your freedom & wealth at any age

(The companion guide to the #1 National Bestseller *How I Retired at 26!*)

Pep Talk

Getting Passed What's Stopping You Right Now!
(audio CD)

(Formally entitled "Making the Rough Places Plain")

1-800-518-ASHA (2742)   •   www.ashatyson.com

About the Author

Asha Tyson is taking the nation by storm while becoming one of America's leading authorities on the development of human potential and personal effectiveness. This success strategist addresses thousands of people on the subjects of personal and professional achievement throughout the United States, Europe, Asia, Australia and Africa.

Her speeches and success materials are described as "dynamic, spellbinding, motivational and inspiring." Her audiences include fortune 500 companies and every size of business and association.

Call today for complete information on booking Asha Tyson to speak at your next meeting, conference or convention. Asha will customize her keynote address, workshop or seminar for your unique needs.

To order copies of *How I Retired at 26!* or to inquire about other Asha Tyson products...

Please Visit:
www.ashatyson.com

For Bookings or Media Interviews Call:
1-800-518-ASHA (2742)